Born to Rise

The Sacred Journey from Mastery to Meaning

From material success to soulful significance — a path to legacy, alignment, and lasting fulfilment.

SHREE SHAMBAV

Born to Rise
The Sacred Journey from Mastery to Meaning
Shree Shambav

Published by Shree Shambav, Tamil Nadu, India

All Rights Reserved

First Edition, 2025

Copyright © 2025, Muniswamy Rajakumar

All rights reserved. No part of this publication may be reproduced, distributed, or transmitted in any form or by any means, including photocopying, recording, or other electronic or mechanical methods, without the author's prior written permission. It is illegal to copy this book, post it to a website, or distribute it by any other means without permission.

The request for permission should be addressed to the author.

ISBN:978-93-343-1831-9
Email:shreeshambav@gmail.com
Web:www.shambav.org

DEDICATION

"Isavasyam idam sarvam yat kim ca jagatyam jagat, tena tyaktena bhunjitha, ma gridhah kasyasvid dhanam"

To the Almighty,

the Divine Masters,

the family who listens,

and my parents who see –

your presence shapes the pages of my life's journey.

"Isavasyam idam sarvam yat kim ca jagatyam jagat"

Meaning: "God encompasses everything you perceive, see, or touch with your sense organs."

DISCLAIMER

This book is a compass, not a commandment.

Born to Rise: The Sacred Journey from Mastery to Meaning is not a manual for perfection, nor is it a blueprint for a single, ideal life. It is a humble offering—an invitation to step beyond the boundaries of ambition and into the quiet, sacred terrain of alignment, legacy, and inner truth.

The reflections and insights within these pages are born from the desire to illuminate paths often forgotten in the noise of the world: the path of soulful success, the courage of integration, and the deep fulfilment that can only emerge when one's outer life harmonises with one's inner voice. This book is not a substitute for professional advice—be it financial, psychological, spiritual, or otherwise. It is not here to define your journey, but to help you listen more deeply to your own.

You may not agree with every idea. That's okay.

This work is not about agreement—it is about awakening. It seeks to stir your conscience, challenge your definitions of worth and wealth, and inspire you to contemplate what it truly means to leave a legacy—not of possessions, but of presence.

Transformation does not come with guarantees. It comes with grace. And grace cannot be taught—it must be welcomed.

Read this book not for instructions, but for illumination. Carry it not as a burden of self-improvement, but as a companion on your sacred return to meaning.

The author and publisher disclaim all liability for any outcomes, direct or indirect, arising from the application of the concepts discussed in this book. By engaging with this material, you acknowledge and accept that personal transformation requires self-responsibility, mindfulness, and discernment.

This book is not a promise of specific results, but an invitation to explore the infinite potential within you. Take what aligns with your journey, leave what does not, and trust in your own capacity for healing, growth, and wisdom.

May this book serve as a catalyst for profound transformation and a deeper understanding of yourself and the world around you.

This is a journey that cannot be measured by milestones, only by moments of truth.

May you not just rise, but rise rooted.

Note - If any part of the book, in any sequence, hurts the reader's sentiments, it would be just out of a sheer accident not intentional

EPIGRAM

Born to Rise

"You were never just meant to build a life —

you were meant to become a light.

Success may elevate you in the world,

but only meaning will illuminate your soul."

— Shree Shambav

Born to Rise

The Sacred Journey from Mastery to Meaning

Shree Shambav

Shree Shambav is a 40x best-selling author renowned for his transformative works in personal development and spiritual growth.

Dear Cherished Readers

Dear Cherished Readers,

As I embark on this new literary voyage, my heart swells with profound gratitude and an overwhelming sense of connection. With deep emotion, I extend my heartfelt appreciation to each of you who has joined me on this journey.

With sincere warmth, I invite you to revisit the steps we have taken together through the pages of my earlier works. Our odyssey began with "Journey of Soul - Karma," a book that marked my first foray into the world of words and a testament to the raw passion that ignited my writing adventure.

The subsequent chapters of our shared journey unfolded through the enchanting tapestry of the *"Twenty + One"* series. With each page turned, it felt as though a brushstroke was added to the canvas of our collective imagination—stories and sentiments woven to echo within the quiet corners of your heart. These weren't just words; they were invitations to feel, to reflect, and to remember what truly matters.

And how can I not cherish the transformative path we walked together through the *"Life Changing Journey—Inspirational Quotes Series?"* Day by day, quote by quote, we ventured inward—into spaces often overlooked—to find wisdom in simplicity and light in life's shadows. Each reflection was offered as a gentle whisper of hope, a spark meant to uplift, inspire, and remind us that even in silence, the soul speaks.

The release of "Death - Light of Life and the Shadow of Death" promises to shed new light on the timeless mystery of death.

The **Optimum Python Series** is a comprehensive guide designed to empower readers at every stage of their programming journey. It begins with *Series I: Ultimate Guide for Beginners*, which lays a strong foundation in Python, making it accessible and engaging for newcomers. *Series II: Exploring Data Structures and Algorithms* takes the next step, offering a deep dive into core computer science principles that enhance problem-solving skills and coding efficiency. Building on this, *Series III: Python Power for Data Science* introduces powerful libraries such as NumPy, Pandas, Matplotlib, and Scikit-learn, guiding readers through data manipulation, visualisation, and foundational machine learning techniques. Finally, *Series IV: Unleashing the Potential of Data Science with Machine Learning Techniques* explores advanced machine learning models and real-world applications, enabling readers to harness the full potential of data-driven insights. Whether you're just starting out or looking to master sophisticated tools and strategies, this series is your roadmap to Python proficiency and beyond.

Shree Shambav expands his artistic repertoire with "*Whispers of Eternity: 150 Plus - A Symphony of Soulful Verses,*" a heartfelt exploration of the human experience. Alongside this, his "*Whispers of the Soul: A Journey Through Haiku*" distils profound insights into poignant verses. Together, these works showcase his versatility and mastery of soulful expression, inviting readers on a journey of self-discovery. Through his poetry, he weaves a rich tapestry of emotion that resonates deeply with the heart.

Shree Shambav's latest works—*Learn to Love Yourself: A Journey of Discovering Inner Beauty and Strength Through 10 Transformative Rules, The Power of Letting Go: Embrace Freedom and Happiness, A Journey of Lasting Peace*—are true treasures of self-discovery, *The Entitlement Trap: Get Over It, Get On, Whispers of a Dying Soul: Unspoken Regrets and Unlived Dreams, Whispers of Silence - Unlocking Inner Power through Stillness, The Power of Words: Transforming Speech, Transforming Lives, The Art of Intentional Living: Minimalism for a Life of Purpose, Awakening the Infinite:The Power of Consciousness in Transforming Life, Beyond the Veil: A Journey Through Life After Death series, Bonds Beyond Blood - Where love builds bridges, and bonds defy blood., A Journey into Spiritual Maturity - 12 Golden Rules for Inner Transformation, The Seeker's Gold : Unlocking Life's Greatest Treasure and The Power of Manifestation - Unlocking The Path From Thought To Reality.*

In addition to these works, Shree Shambav has recently ventured into astrology with the release of Astrology Unveiled – Foundations of Ancient Wisdom Series I to VI, expanding into the realm of metaphysics. These books explore the foundational principles of Vedic astrology, offering readers a rich and practical understanding of this ancient wisdom.

Your unwavering support, enthusiasm to immerse yourself in my writings, and readiness to embark on these journeys with me have been my greatest sources of inspiration. Your input has been a beacon guiding me through the creation process, moulding these stories into containers of passion, emotion, knowledge, and resonance.

As I unveil this new narrative before you, know that your presence, insights, and shared moments have been my companions. The path we have walked together is etched in the annals of my creative evolution, and it's an honour beyond words to have you by my side once more.

Here's to the readers who have illuminated my path with their presence, who have embraced my stories with open hearts, and who have woven themselves into the very fabric of my literary world. Our journey has been a symbiotic dance of writer and reader, a harmony of souls brought together by the magic of storytelling.

With a heart brimming with appreciation and eyes glistening with anticipation, I extend my deepest gratitude for your unwavering support. Thank you for the memories, the shared emotions, and the countless hours spent in the worlds we've crafted together. As we step into this new adventure, let's continue to explore, feel, and discover the boundless horizons that words can unveil.

Warmly,

Shree Shambav

Suggested Reads

Endorsements

"**Born to Rise – The Sacred Journey from Mastery to Meaning is not just a book — it's a soul-awakening experience.**

Shree Shambav masterfully guides us beyond the surface of success into the depths of what it means to live with purpose, integrity, and soul. This book speaks to those who have 'arrived' in the world's eyes but still feel an unspoken longing for something more—something enduring, something real.

With poetic precision and profound insight, Shree peels back the layers of material mastery to reveal the essence of a life well-lived. He reminds us that wealth without wisdom is hollow, and that true legacy is born not from what we accumulate, but from what we *integrate* and *embody*.

This is the rare kind of work that doesn't just inform — it transforms.

A sacred guide for those ready to shift from ambition to alignment, from striving to soulful significance. A must-read for anyone who's ever achieved 'success' and found themselves quietly asking, *What now?*

This book will meet you where you are — and invite you to rise again… this time, from the inside out."

SHREE SHAMBAV

— Rohith, Advocate

About the Author

Shree Shambav is an internationally acclaimed best-selling author, inspirational speaker, artist, philanthropist, life coach, strategist and entrepreneur. A world record holder, his deep passion for music led him to create soul-stirring albums, drawing inspiration from his celebrated poetry collection, Whispers of Eternity. His profound insights have sparked deep personal transformations, guiding countless individuals toward self-discovery, purposeful living, and authenticity.

With an extraordinary ability to unlock human potential, Shree empowers individuals to break through limitations and embrace their highest selves. His writings, lectures, and compassionate guidance continue to uplift lives, fostering resilience, mindfulness, and personal growth.

Shree Shambav is a 40x best-selling author celebrated for his profound contributions to personal development and spiritual growth.

Shree Shambav's literary journey took flight with the celebrated Journey of Soul - Karma, where he delved into the depths of human experience to unveil profound insights. Garnering recognition through multiple literature awards, his repertoire includes esteemed works, such as the Twenty + One Series, and the enlightening Life Changing Journey – Inspirational Quotes series.

As a distinguished alumnus of the Indian Institute of Management and the National Institute of Technology, Shree Shambav brings a wealth of corporate acumen from his tenure in multinational corporations. His most recent publications, including Unveiling the Enigma, Death - Light of Life and the Shadow of Death and Optimum – Power Python Series I, Series II, Series III and Series IV, demonstrate his mastery of both the literary and technical spheres.

Shree Shambav expands his artistic repertoire with "*Whispers of Eternity: 150 Plus - A Symphony of Soulful Verses*," a heartfelt exploration of the human experience. Alongside this, his "*Whispers of the Soul: A Journey Through Haiku*" distils profound insights into poignant verses. Together, these works showcase his versatility and mastery of soulful expression, inviting readers on a journey of self-discovery. Through his poetry, he weaves a rich tapestry of emotion that resonates deeply with the heart.

Shree Shambav's latest works—*Learn to Love Yourself: A Journey of Discovering Inner Beauty and Strength Through 10 Transformative*

Rules, The Power of Letting Go: Embrace Freedom and Happiness, A Journey of Lasting Peace—are true treasures of self-discovery, *The Entitlement Trap: Get Over It, Get On, Whispers of a Dying Soul: Unspoken Regrets and Unlived Dreams, Whispers of Silence - Unlocking Inner Power through Stillness, The Power of Words: Transforming Speech, Transforming Lives, The Art of Intentional Living: Minimalism for a Life of Purpose, Awakening the Infinite:The Power of Consciousness in Transforming Life, Beyond the Veil: A Journey Through Life After Death series, Bonds Beyond Blood - Where love builds bridges, and bonds defy blood., A Journey into Spiritual Maturity - 12 Golden Rules for Inner Transformation, The Seeker's Gold : Unlocking Life's Greatest Treasure and The Power of Manifestation - Unlocking The Path From Thought To Reality.*

In addition to these works, Shree Shambav has recently ventured into astrology with the release of Astrology Unveiled – Foundations of Ancient Wisdom Series I to VI, expanding into the realm of metaphysics. These books explore the foundational principles of Vedic astrology, offering readers a rich and practical understanding of this ancient wisdom.

Shree Shambav established the Ayur Rakshita Foundation, which is dedicated to promoting boundless growth, universal fraternity, and environmental protection. The charity helps diverse communities while working for societal progress.

To learn more about Shree Shambav and his works, visit his website at www.shambav.org. For information about the Ayur Rakshita Foundation and its initiatives, visit www.shambav-ayurrakshita.org.

Let's Follow him on Social Media: **@shreeshambav**

Main: https://linktr.ee/shreeshambav

SHREE SHAMBAV

Website: https://www.shambav.org/

LinkedIn: https://www.linkedin.com/in/shreeshambav/

Blog: https://blog.shambav.org/

Instagram: https://www.instagram.com/shreeshambav/

YouTube: https://www.youtube.com/@shreeshambav

Amazon: https://www.amazon.com/author/shreeshambav

Goodreads: https://www.goodreads.com/author/show/22367436.Shree_Shambav

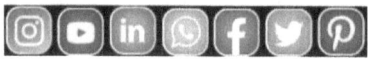

PREFACE

"True wealth begins when we stop chasing and start becoming."

- Shree Shambav

Preface:

Continuing the Journey Within

A Threshold Between Worlds

There comes a moment—subtle but seismic—when the echo of external success begins to fade, and a quieter longing starts to speak from within. It does not shout. It does not clamour. It simply asks:

"Is this all there is?"

"Have I climbed the right mountain?"

"What now, when the world calls me 'successful,' but my soul craves something more?"

If you are holding this book now, chances are—you've already walked a meaningful stretch of the outer path. You've built. You've earned. You've achieved. You've learned how to play the game of mastery in the material world.

Book One, *Born to Rise: The Unspoken Principles Behind Power, Riches, and Lasting Wealth*, was your compass in that terrain. It gave you clarity on what power, wealth, and riches truly mean—not as symbols, but as forces. You cultivated a mindset, strategy, and internal strength. You shed illusions and began to define success on your own terms.

But this next ascent is not about *more*.

It is about *meaning*.

The Shift Has Already Begun

You may have noticed it: the subtle ache during celebrations that should've felt fulfilling. The way your ambition no longer sparks fire but starts to feel like fatigue. The truth that certain relationships, achievements, or goals—once magnetic—now feel misaligned.

This is not a failure.

This is your *awakening*.

Not a detour, but the divine unfolding of your rise.

To truly *rise*, the soul must come with you.

The outer climb may earn you recognition.

But it is the **inner ascent** that brings remembrance.

Remembrance of why you began.

Remembrance of who you truly are beneath the roles, rewards, and rhythms.

Remembrance that **success was never the destination**—only the doorway to a deeper way of being.

Mastery Was Just the Beginning

This book is not for the seeker of quick wins. It is for the one willing to sit in silence long enough to hear the sacred.

It is for the one ready to ask:

- What does a *meaningful* life look like now?
- How do I turn mastery into **contribution**, riches into **legacy**, and strategy into **wisdom**?
- What must I *unlearn* in order to live fully?
- And how can my *inner alignment* become the greatest force I've ever built?

These are not business questions. These are soul questions. And they mark the sacred terrain ahead.

What This Book Is—and Is Not

This book will not teach you how to acquire more.

It will show you how to **become more**.

It will not ask you to hustle harder.

It will ask you to listen deeper.

It will not hand you a blueprint.

It will hold up a **mirror**.

A mirror to your values.

To your gifts.

To the **legacy only you** can leave.

Each chapter is a gateway—not just into ideas, but into *integration*.

You will walk through Alignment.

You will walk through Integration.

You will begin to experience what it means to **live a life that outlives you**.

You Are the Sacred Instrument

You were never just building a business, a brand, or a bank account.

You were building the *container* through which your soul could sing.

Now is the time to tune that instrument.

To find your rhythm again.

To rise—not in noise, but in *depth*.

Not in status, but in **spirit**.

Because true power is peace.

True wealth is wisdom.

And true success is a life aligned—with who you are, what you give, and what you leave behind.

Welcome to the Sacred Journey

This is not just a continuation.

It is a deepening.

An unravelling.

A remembering.

You were not born to just rise.

You were born to rise—and **keep rising***,*

until your very presence becomes your greatest contribution.

Now, we begin again.

Not from the bottom.

But from the **centre***.*

Let the ascent begin.

With gratitude and encouragement,

Shree Shambav

INTRODUCTION

The Silent Forces That Shape Destiny

Every great rise begins in silence.

Not in applause, not in recognition, but in quiet moments of reckoning—where you confront the gap between who you are and who you were meant to become.

Most people spend their lives reacting to the world around them. They chase shadows of success, mimic the moves of others, and build lives that look good but feel hollow. Not because they lack ambition—but because they lack **clarity**. Clarity of what they truly seek. Clarity of what power, riches, and wealth actually mean—not just to society, but to *them*.

This book begins with a truth many overlook:

You are already powerful.

You are already rich in ways the world may never measure. And wealth is not something you chase—it is something you uncover and cultivate from within.

But here's the paradox—these truths remain dormant in most lives, buried beneath the noise of comparison, the fear of not-enough, and the conditioning that tells you to follow instead of forge.

This book is your map back to yourself.

It is not a manual of tactics—it is a journey through the inner architecture that governs your outer results. Because the world doesn't give you what you want. It mirrors who you are. And who you are is shaped by what you believe—about power, about money, about yourself.

So before we build, we must *understand*.

Before we ascend, we must *unlearn*.

And before we accumulate, we must *align*.

In Part I, we will redefine the very landscape you've been taught to navigate—exploring the deeper meanings of power, riches, and wealth. You'll learn why confusing these terms leads to inner conflict, and how clearly seeing their distinctions can liberate your choices.

In Part II, we move inward—to the mindset, psychology, and strategy of those who rise with purpose and stay rooted in fulfilment. This is where we talk about mental mastery, strategic compounding, the hidden emotions behind money, and the silent forces that either drive or derail your destiny.

This book does not promise overnight success.

What it offers is far more valuable: a **foundation**—timeless, internal, and unshakable.

Because power without clarity is dangerous.

Riches without wisdom are fleeting.

And wealth without meaning is just a prettier form of poverty.

You were *born to rise*.

Not merely to succeed, but to lead. Not merely to earn, but to embody.

And this is the first step—to remember who you are, and to reclaim the forces within you that shape your future long before the world sees your rise.

Let us begin—

Not with noise, but with knowing.

— *Shree Shambav*

A New Kind of Rich

Rich in spirit.

Rich in time.

Rich in impact.

Rich in peace.

This is the wealth the world forgets to talk about.

But it is the only kind that truly lasts.

If you feel the pull to live beyond the surface…

If you are tired of the illusions…

If you are ready to build something that the world cannot take from you…

Then this book is your companion.

It's time to rise—not just higher, but deeper.

To not just succeed, but **transcend**.

To not just make a living, but **craft a legacy**.

Welcome to *Born to Rise*.

Let's begin the ascent.

— **Shree Shambav**

PROLOGUE

Before the Rise

When the World Goes Quiet

There are moments in life that don't announce themselves. Moments that arrive without noise or ceremony—yet mark the beginning of everything that follows.

For some, it is a quiet dissatisfaction in the middle of success.

For others, it is the sting of failure, a betrayal, a collapse, or simply a strange emptiness despite achieving all that was once dreamed.

We call it many names—midlife, awakening, breakdown, breakthrough.

But beneath the label lies one simple truth:

Something within you is done pretending.

Done pretending that success alone can fulfil you.

Done pretending that being busy means being important.
Done pretending that following the rules will lead to freedom.

In that silence—raw and unfiltered—you begin to see with new eyes.

You begin to ask the deeper questions:

What am I really building?

Whose definition of power am I chasing?

Is this wealth… or just a collection of well-decorated fears?

This book was born from that silence.

Not the kind found in isolation, but the kind that follows awakening.

You see, the world will teach you to run—faster, harder, louder.

It rarely teaches you how to **rise**—with intention, alignment, and inner clarity.

It celebrates those who "make it," but forgets to ask: *Make it to what? And at what cost?*

So before we chase another goal, we must pause. Before we climb higher, we must ask: *Is the ladder leaning on the right wall?*

Because power, when misunderstood, becomes control.

Riches, when untethered from purpose, become anxiety.

And wealth, without inner clarity, becomes a golden cage—impressive from the outside, but hollow within.

But power, when rooted in purpose, becomes presence.

Riches, when guided by meaning, become impact.

And wealth, when aligned with the soul, becomes legacy.

This book is your invitation to that deeper path.

Not a rejection of material mastery, but a redefinition of it.

Not a denial of ambition, but a refinement of it.

Not an escape from the world, but a return to your truest self *within* it.

Here, you will find the **foundations** of a new way to rise—

A way where clarity is the compass, mindset is the engine, and fulfilment is not postponed until the end, but woven into every step of the journey.

So let this be the moment where the world goes quiet…

And something eternal within you begins to speak.

You were not just born to survive.

Not just born to succeed.

You were born to rise.

And the time has come.

— *Shree Shambav*

CONTENTS

DEDICATION iii
DISCLAIMER v
EPIGRAM vii
Dear Cherished Readers xi
Suggested Reads xv
Endorsements xvii
About the Author xix
PREFACE xxiii
INTRODUCTION xxix
A New Kind of Rich xxxiii
PROLOGUE xxxv
CONTENTS xxxix
PART ONE 41
CHAPTER I 43
   Mastering the Material World 43
CHAPTER II 71
   Intellectual Assets and Invisible Capital 71
CHAPTER III 99
   The Energetics of Wealth 99
PART TWO 121
   INTEGRATION — Living a Life that Outlives You . 121

CHAPTER IV 123
Legacy that Outlives You 123
CHAPTER V 147
Relationships and Social Capital 147
CHAPTER VI 175
From Breakdown to Breakthrough 175
CHAPTER VII 203
Rituals of the Wealthy and Wise 203
Final Chapter 229
Becoming the Architect of Your Destiny 229
WRAP UP 255
Rise, and Keep Rising 255
APPENDICES 281
APPENDICES A 283
Actionable Insights & Tools 283
Life Coach and Philanthropist 291
TESTIMONIALS 293
ACKNOWLEDGEMENTS 301

PART ONE

ALIGNMENT - From Material to Meaning

"When your earning, saving, and spending reflect your values, the material world bows to you—not the other way around."

-Shree Shambav

CHAPTER I

Mastering the Material World

"Mastery begins the moment you can let go of what you own—and still take care of it."

— Shree Shambav

Synopsis

Mastering the Material World redefines success—not as accumulation, but as alignment. This section teaches how to own without being owned, to possess without being possessed. From the discipline of detached ownership to building automated systems that generate income in your absence, the focus shifts from hustle to harmony. Here, earning, saving, and spending become spiritual expressions of self-awareness. True mastery arises not from control, but from clarity—understanding the purpose behind your money and the energy behind every transaction. This path offers not only financial sustainability, but also soulful satisfaction.

The Art of Holding Lightly

— *On Wealth, Ownership, and the Sacred Space Between*

The Monk and the Mansion

In the lush hills of Rishikesh, there lived a man named **Daksh**, once a high-powered executive in the city, who had traded his suits for silence and skyscrapers for sunrise. But unlike the monks in saffron who walked barefoot through the forest, Daksh still owned a house—a beautiful, serene hilltop mansion made of stone and cedar, adorned with handwoven rugs, and filled with books and art.

Visitors often asked him:

"How can you live like a monk in a mansion?"

"Isn't this attachment?"

Daksh would smile gently and say,

"The house is mine to care for. But not mine to *cling* to."

"Ownership is responsibility. Attachment is imprisonment."

The Paradox: Having Without Being Had

Most people believe detachment means renunciation—giving everything away, owning nothing, living with empty hands. But **true detachment is not the absence of possession—it is the absence of *possession over the soul*.**

You can have wealth, art, cars, land, and legacy…

…but if they *own your mind*, you are not free.

"It's not the thing itself, but how you hold it, that defines your inner state."

A sword in the hand of a warrior is protection.

The same sword in the hands of a fearful man is a danger.

Similarly, money in the hands of the unattached is a tool.

Money in the hands of the bound becomes a chain.

The Steward and the Storm

Imagine you are **a steward of a beautiful garden**.

You water the trees, trim the roses, and pull the weeds.

You love the garden—but deep in your heart, you know:

The land is not yours. It belongs to time.

One day, a storm may come.

A tree might fall.

A drought may wither the blooms.

But you are not shattered, because you were never *possessive*.

You were *devoted*.

"You are not the owner. You are the caretaker. And love without clinging is the highest form of love."

This is what it means to manage wealth **with detachment**—to give your best to your craft, your business, your estate, while knowing that **none of it is permanent**, and **none of it defines you**.

Why This Balance Is Vital for Inner Freedom

1. **Attachment breeds anxiety. Stewardship cultivates peace.**

When you're attached, every dip in the market shakes your identity.

When you're a steward, you respond with calm, because you understand cycles.

2. **Possession inflates the ego. Detachment humbles the spirit.**

    You start believing you are what you own. But what happens when it's gone?

3. **Detachment allows generosity.**

    You can give more, because you're not giving yourself away.

    A hand that grips cannot give. A hand that opens—blesses.

4. **It frees your creativity.**

    You stop building from fear. You start creating with purpose.

Practising Detachment in Material Life: Practical Pathways

1. Ritualise Gratitude Without Clinging

- Bless your home daily. But whisper: "This is not forever."
- Drive your car with care. But know: "I am not my car."

- Receive income with joy. But say: "This flows *through* me, not *to* me."

2. Name What You Fear Losing—and Surrender It

- Write down what you're most attached to.
- Ask: *What does this item say about me?*
- Ask: *Who am I without it?*
- Then say: **"Even if this leaves me, I remain whole."**

"The art of detachment is not rejection. It is release."

Like letting a bird rest on your shoulder—without caging it.

3. Create a Sacred Space Between You and Your Wealth

- Make decisions about money from stillness, not from neediness.
- Budget with consciousness, not control.
- Invest with wisdom, not obsession.

4. Give Something Away—Regularly

- Not just old clothes. Give something that feels meaningful.
- Train your nervous system to feel **safe without grasping.**
- Feel the emptiness. Then feel the lightness.

The Fire and the Flame

In the Vedic texts, there's a metaphor of the **householder yogi**—a person who lives in the world fully, yet walks through it as if **wearing a silk robe in a room of fire**—aware, awake, careful not to let the robe catch.

He or she cooks meals, raises children, earns wealth, and builds a legacy—not out of ego or fear, but out of love.

"You can light the fire. Just don't become the flame."

Let your wealth serve your soul. Not the other way around.

Back to Daksh...

Years later, after a flood washed through the valley, Daksh's house stood damaged. When friends came running in, worried, he smiled and served tea amidst the soaked floorboards.

"I'll rebuild," he said. "But nothing was truly lost."

They looked at him in awe.

"Because I lived in the house," he explained,

"But the house never lived in me."

When the River Flows Without You

— On Building Systems That Work While You Rest

The Beginning: The Tired Builder

In the early chapters of his life, **Arup** was like many of us—**a builder who never stopped building.** He worked hard, built a business from scratch, handled every transaction, every client call, every emergency. He took pride in being "hands-on."

*But quietly, behind the victories, **his soul was tired.***

He had created income, yes. But not freedom.

Every rupee was earned by trade—his time for money.

Vacations felt like theft from his own business.

Rest felt like risk.

Until one day, while sitting at the edge of the Ganga in silence, watching the river move, he whispered something that would change everything:

"If this river can flow without anyone pushing it…

why can't my life?"

The Shift: From Labour to Leverage

This moment began a transformation in Arup. He realised that while he had built **a strong business**, he had not built **a strong system.**

A system doesn't just generate money.

A true system generates **freedom, continuity,** and **peace— even in your absence.**

He began asking a different question:

"How can I build something that serves me—even while I sleep, rest, or walk away?"

This wasn't just about automation.

It was about *alignment.*

The Windmill vs. the Treadmill

Imagine two men:

- One runs on a **treadmill.**

The faster he runs, the more energy he burns. But the moment he stops, everything halts. He mistakes motion for progress.

- The other builds a **windmill.**

It takes time. It feels slow at first. But once built, the wind itself works for him—he channels nature's flow into energy.

Arup had been on the treadmill.

Now, he was learning to build windmills.

What Does It Truly Mean to Build Systems That Serve You?

1. It means designing *repeatable engines*, not heroic effort.

- A bakery where every morning Arup had to be there at 5 AM to open was not a system.

- But a bakery with a trained team, digital ordering, supplier automation, and trusted leadership *was* a system.

"If it needs you every day, it owns you."

2. It means investing in processes, people, and platforms.

He started investing not just in profits, but in **people** who could make decisions without him.

He documented workflows, empowered others, and removed himself from being the bottleneck.

"Freedom comes not from more effort, but from *better design*."

3. It means your money starts to work harder than you do.

Arup began setting up systems in his **personal finances,** too.

- Auto-investments.
- Diversified income streams.
- Passive revenue from digital products, books, and royalties.
- Real estate with a trusted manager.

Money was no longer earned only when he was awake.

It was earned while he was meditating.

While he was reading.

While he was caring for his ageing parents.

While he was simply *being*.

Redefining Financial Independence

The old belief was:

"I'll be financially free when I earn X amount."

But Arup learned the deeper truth:

"You're free when your life supports you—**without you constantly supporting it.**"

Financial independence is not a number.

It's a structure.

It's when your **income is not tied to exhaustion.**

When **systems protect you from chaos.**

When **time becomes yours again.**

A Deeper Layer: Systems as Spiritual Practice

Building systems is not just a technical pursuit.

It is a **sacred responsibility**—to your future self, your family, and your mission.

"You do not build systems so you can be lazy.

You build them so you can live *fully*."

With systems:

- You write more poetry.

- You take long walks with your child.
- You care for your health, your spirit, and your purpose.
- You teach. You mentor. You rest without guilt.

Systems free the soul to rise above survival.

Arup at the Ganga, Again

Ten years later, Arup sits at the same bend in the river.

He is no longer watching in longing.

He is **living in flow**.

His businesses continue without his micromanagement.

His finances grow quietly.

His calendar has space—*space to think, breathe, love.*

A young man approaches him and asks: **"How did you achieve this peace?"**

Arup smiles and says:

"I stopped working *on* the river.

I started working *like* the river."

"Now, the systems carry me—just as the river carries the leaf."

"Grace is not just divine. Grace is also *designed.*"

Reflection

To build systems is to build rhythm into your life.

To replace panic with planning.

To build something that lasts beyond your mood, beyond your health, beyond your presence.

It is not a betrayal of effort—it is the **highest expression of intelligence.**

Because life is not meant to be managed.

It is meant to be **lived.**

The Symphony of Gold: When Money Learns to Breathe

— *On Balancing Spending, Saving, and Earning*

Act I: The Dissonance

Arup had once thought he was doing everything right.

He earned handsomely.

He saved diligently.

He spent cautiously.

And yet—something inside felt misaligned.

Every time he bought something he enjoyed, guilt knocked at the door.

Every time he saved, he feared it would never be enough.

Every time he earned, he felt he was trading his life for numbers.

From the outside, it looked like **success.**

From the inside, it felt like **suppression.**

The Music of Breath

A wise mentor once told Arup over a late evening tea:

"Arup, money is like breath—

You must *receive* (earn),

You must *retain* (save),

And you must *release* (spend).

If you hold any part too long, you suffocate."

That was the turning point.

He realised:

He had been **inhaling wealth** with no space to exhale.

Or at other times, **exhaling through spending** to feel alive, without knowing why he couldn't hold on to it.

What he lacked wasn't income or intelligence.

What he lacked was **inner harmony** with money's rhythm.

Act II: The Three Pillars—Earn, Save, Spend

Let us dive into each dimension and how imbalance turns gold into grief.

1. Earning Without Purpose → Emptiness in Achievement

Arup once chased earnings for the thrill of "more." Promotions. Milestones. Bigger numbers.

But unchecked **earning**—driven by fear, greed, or ego—**burns the soul.**

You become like a man **digging wells in every direction**, hoping to find water. You exhaust yourself, yet never taste depth.

Without purpose, earning becomes an addiction.

You don't know when to stop. You don't know *why* you started.

2. Saving Without Joy → Scarcity in Abundance

There was a time Arup had saved for years—out of anxiety, out of inherited trauma, out of generational echoes of "what if?"

His bank account grew.

His heart shrank.

He skipped small pleasures. He withheld generosity. He postponed joy.

He realised one day, when looking at an old, unused travel voucher:

"What am I saving for, if I forget how to live?"

Savings are not a fortress.

They are a *bridge*—a protector of future freedom.

But when savings come from fear, they enslave.

3. Spending Without Awareness → Pleasure Without Peace

In his younger years, Arup spent to feel seen.

He bought gifts he couldn't afford, clothes that he wore rather than the other way around, and dinners that numbed the hunger for something deeper.

Spending became a drug. A proxy for love.

He once told himself, "I deserve this," when what he really meant was, "I need to feel enough."

Spending without soul is like pouring water into sand.

No matter how much you give it, it disappears.

Act III: The Return to Balance

With time, reflection, and honest conversation with himself, Arup found a new way of being—what he called **"The Financial Triveni"**, named after the holy confluence of three sacred rivers.

Just as **Ganga, Yamuna, and Saraswati** met in silent union—so too, his money practices began to flow together:

- **He earned from his zone of purpose.** From what he *loved*, not just what paid. This brought joy.

- **He saved not out of fear, but as a sacred act of self-love.** This brought security.

- **He spent mindfully, in alignment with his values—not his insecurities.** This brought peace.

The Mirror Within

Arup began to notice something miraculous:

- His relationships softened.

- His health improved.
- He stopped comparing.
- He no longer felt the need to prove anything.

Why?

Because **money was no longer noise.**

It had become music.

And the song it sang was **inner harmony.**

When One Aspect Dominates…

- When you only earn but never spend: you forget to live.
- When you only save but never give: you forget to love.
- When you only spend but never earn mindfully: you forget to grow.

An imbalance in money is never just about finances.

It **echoes a spiritual imbalance**—an absence of trust, an over-identification with control, or a rejection of self-worth.

"How you do money… is often how you do life."

Reflection: Your Symphony Awaits

You are not meant to be a prisoner of one chord.

You are not meant to inhale without exhaling.

You are a being of flow. Of rhythm. Of movement.

Let your **earnings be a dance with purpose**,
Your **savings be an embrace of your future**,
And your **spending be a celebration of the now.**
And when all three move in harmony—
Money no longer owns you. It serves you.
It stops being currency—and becomes clarity.

The Monk Who Rebuilt the Market

— *Why Mastering the Material World is a Spiritual and Strategic Act*

Act I: The Tension Between Two Worlds

Arup once sat at the edge of a quiet mountain lake, a journal in hand, heart heavy with a question:

"Do I need to renounce the world to find peace—or must I master it to live in truth?"

He had spent years walking the corporate halls of power—well-groomed, well-paid, and well-acknowledged.

But within, he carried a growing ache.

He had meditated with monks.

He had earned bonuses that could buy silence.

Yet the silence never stayed.

He was torn between two false extremes:

- The **illusion of detachment**: believing that true spirituality meant rejecting the material.

- The **illusion of domination**: believing that control over material assets guarantees fulfilment.

Neither had satisfied his soul.

Act II: The Wake-Up Call

It wasn't until Arup visited his childhood village during a festival that something shifted.

He saw his uncle—once a humble farmer—now running a thriving co-operative, with dignity and depth.

The man wore no saffron robes. He quoted no scriptures. But his life radiated alignment.

When Arup asked him the secret, the old man smiled:

"Spirituality isn't about escaping money. It's about teaching it where to kneel."

"Make money your servant—not your master. And let your values sign its paycheck."

That day, something ancient and powerful woke inside Arup.

The Sword and the Monk

Imagine a monk walking through a kingdom.

He is wise, composed, kind—but unarmed in a world that respects power.

Then imagine a warrior with a gleaming sword—but no clarity of heart. He may win battles, but he will lose himself.

But what happens when the monk **learns to wield the sword?**

When he sees it not as a weapon of ego, but as a tool of service?

That is what money becomes when mastered: a sacred blade in the hands of an awakened being.

Why Mastering the Material is Spiritual

Here's what most miss:

1. **Money reveals your shadows.**

   It exposes where you feel not enough. Where you cling. Where you hide?

   Mastering it demands confronting your deepest emotional patterns: comparison, scarcity, shame, and pride.

2. **Wealth tests your soul's integrity.**

   With more comes the temptation to dominate, to detach, to distort truth for convenience.

   If you can stay anchored in values while navigating wealth—you're living with mastery.

3. **Resources enable ripple effects.**

   You can't build schools on good intentions alone. You can't lift your family from a generational struggle with only poetry.

   Money—when aligned—is the megaphone of mission.

4. **Order in the outer reflects order in the inner.**

   Clarity in finances, stewardship, and systems reflects your inner discipline, attention, and vision.

The Buddha sat under a Bodhi tree. But his teachings moved through empires because kings funded monasteries and merchants supported the Sangha.

Act III: How Arup Aligned the Two Worlds

Back in the city, Arup didn't quit his job.

He **redefined it**.

- He clarified his *why*—shifting from accumulation to contribution.

- He automated his finances—not to escape responsibility, but to free mental space.

- He created **value systems** for his spending and giving: each rupee a reflection of inner intention.

- He built **assets that could serve him and others, even in rest**—investments, content, and people.

He started to **lead teams like a gardener**—*not a general.*

He mentored not for credit, but legacy.

He earned without anxiety. Spent without guilt. Gave without fear.

And most importantly—**he slept without weight.**

So How Can One Start This Alignment—Today?

Let's be practical, grounded, and deep:

1. Name Your Intentions

Before the budget or the business plan—ask:

What kind of human do I want to become? What will money help me protect, express, or offer?

Your answer is your compass. Without this, wealth becomes a wandering ghost.

2. Audit Emotional Leaks

Where does your energy leak around money?

- Fear of checking accounts?
- Guilt in spending on yourself?
- Resentment in giving?

Track the feelings—not just the figures.

Healing begins with awareness.

3. Design Systems with Soul

Spiritual alignment doesn't mean disorganised.

Create conscious systems:

- Auto-investing toward freedom.
- Sacred budgets for giving.

- Calendared silence and solitude—because time is also wealth.

4. Own and Release Simultaneously

Practice **detached stewardship**:

Own without clinging.

Grow without hoarding.

Plan without worshiping control.

Like tending a garden—you till, water, and prune. But you don't shout at the tree to grow faster.

5. Surround Yourself with Embodied Models

Find people who've walked this bridge between the sacred and the strategic. Learn from their inner posture, not just their outer success.

Success is energy. It's felt before it's copied.

Reflection: The Real Wealth

At the end of his life, Arup didn't remember all the zeros.

He remembered the **sense of peace** as he gave his daughter her first financial journal.

He remembered the **warmth** of a stranger thanking him for funding their art school.

He remembered his own trembling hands signing a will that reflected every value he ever stood for.

That—was mastery.

Not because he had money.

But because he knew who he was—with it, without it, beyond it.

True wealth is not measured by what you hold—but by what flows through you without breaking your spirit.

You are not meant to shun the material.

You are meant to **bless it. Shape it. Wield it. Release it.**

That is the sacred art of material mastery.

The Sacred Steward's Framework

A Ritual-Based Practice for Material Mastery and Inner Harmony

Daily Ritual — *"The Mirror & The Map"*

A morning and evening practice to align inner peace with outer stewardship

Time: 10–15 minutes

Tools: Journal, candle or sacred object, quiet space

Morning: The Map (Setting Direction)

1. **Light a candle / touch a grounding object.**

    "I welcome clarity and truth in all I do today."

2. **Ask:**

- How do I want to feel while earning today?
- What one financial decision can I make in alignment with who I'm becoming?

3. **Visualise:**

See money flowing like a river through your hands—nourishing needs, lifting others, never stagnant.

4. **Affirm:**

"I create from wholeness. I receive with grace. I spend with my soul."

Evening: The Mirror (Reflect & Recalibrate)

1. **Ask yourself honestly:**
    - Did my actions reflect my deepest values today?
    - Where did fear, guilt, or ego show up around money or possessions?
    - Where did love, confidence, or wisdom lead me?

2. **Forgive & Affirm:**
    - *"I release what no longer serves. I am learning. I am sovereign."*

3. **Gratitude List:**
    - One thing you earned with integrity.

- One thing you spent joyfully or gave freely.
- One moment of spiritual alignment.

Weekly Practice — *"Stewardship Sunday"*

A sacred hour to manage, review, and bless your financial life with intention.

Time: 1 hour, once a week

Tools: Notebook or financial dashboard, tea or incense, quiet space

1. **Bless Your Finances:**

    Light a candle, whisper:

    "May these resources reflect love, wisdom, and purpose."

2. **The Three-Lens Review:**
    - **Spending:** Did I use money to nurture my values and vitality?
    - **Saving:** Did I honour my future self?
    - **Earning:** Did I create value with presence and dignity?

3. **Recalibrate Systems:**
    - Adjust budgets or flows if needed.
    - Move money consciously (not reactively).

- Schedule upcoming contributions or generosity.

4. **Soul Ledger:**
    - Where did I feel rich beyond money?
    - Where did I feel poor despite it?

5. **Vision Refresh:**
    - Revisit your long-term *"Why"*.
    - Journal a paragraph that starts with:

"I am building a legacy where…"

Monthly Ceremony — *"The Alignment Audit"*

A deeper practice to ensure your financial path aligns with your spiritual truth.

Time: 1.5–2 hours

Timing: New Moon or Full Moon

1. **Silence (15 min):**
2. Sit in silence. Observe your breath. Let the surface mind settle.
3. **Write:**
    - What am I clinging to materially that no longer brings peace?

- What fear is still driving some of my earning or saving habits?
- What would my most spiritually aligned self do with wealth?

4. **Recommit:**

    - Update your vision board or personal manifesto.
    - Let go of one material item or expense you've outgrown.
    - Plan one act of generosity with full presence.

Long-Term Alignment Framework

Create systems that honour rest, value, and service

Pillar	Description	Example
Earning with Soul	Build income from aligned service.	Coaching, creative work, and business with ethics
Spending with Sincerity	Conscious consumption rooted in values	"Is this purchase supporting who I want to be?"
Saving with Wisdom	Protect your future self with care, not fear	Emergency fund, goal-based savings
Investing with Intention	Money in motion that creates long-term value	Ethical funds, real estate, skill-building
Giving with Grace	Offering back from fullness, not obligation	Monthly giving ritual, time or energy support
Resting with Trust	Letting systems work while you rejuvenate	Passive income, time-off planning, and automation

Your Inner Mantra for Material Mastery:

"I am not here to escape the material world. I am here to inhabit it with such sacred presence that even money bows to truth."

CHAPTER II

Intellectual Assets and Invisible Capital

"When your knowledge becomes someone else's transformation, you've entered the realm of lasting wealth."

– Shree Shambav

Synopsis

Intellectual Assets and Invisible Capital illuminates the silent power behind the world's most influential people: their ability to create, share, and scale ideas. This section explores how knowledge, content, reputation, and unique perspective—when properly framed—become invaluable currencies in the digital and entrepreneurial age. Whether it's a book, a brand, or a breakthrough idea, your inner world can be externalised into real-world value. This path is not just about monetisation, but about magnification—turning thoughts into tools, and wisdom into wealth. The chapter empowers you to build quietly powerful empires from within.

The Silent Forge: How the Invisible Becomes Irreplaceable"

The Old World and the Forgotten Smith

In a quiet mountain village, there once lived a blacksmith named Harry. Known for neither speed nor scale, his forge was small — barely visible on the trading maps. But his creations were legendary. Every blade he crafted carried something no machine could replicate — a whisper of soul, a song of struggle, and a story only time could polish.

Merchants would travel for weeks not for quantity, but for quality. Not for efficiency, but for meaning. What they bought wasn't iron—it was **essence**. They trusted not the blade, but the **man behind the fire**.

As time passed, the world changed. Gold outshone craft. Mass replaced mastery. Markets grew taller than mountains. Yet whispers of Harry's legacy still circled like wind in the trees.

Why?

Because the **value created from the soul is never obsolete**. It outlives trends. It outlasts steel.

And in today's world, the forges have gone digital. But the principle remains the same.

Modern Wealth is Rooted in the Invisible

Today, we live in an **idea-driven economy** — where:

- A tweet can spark a revolution.

- A podcast can generate more trust than a thousand ads.

- A single article can change the course of a career.

- A personal brand — authentic and consistent — can become more powerful than a billion-dollar company with no face.

Welcome to the age of **invisible architecture** — where **ideas, content, and reputation** are the bricks that build modern castles.

Let's break it down:

1. Ideas: The Seeds of Asymmetrical Wealth

Ideas are **leverage points**.

One good idea — properly planted — can:

- Attract attention.

- Solve problems.

- Build movements.

- Birth businesses.

Analogy:
An idea is like a mango seed. To the untrained eye, it's just a pit. But to a farmer, it's an orchard. To a visionary, it's a legacy. The seed doesn't shout — but when nurtured, it **feeds generations**.

In a world of noise, originality is currency.

2. Content: The Bridge Between Thought and Trust

You can have the best ideas, but if no one knows, they rot inside.

Content is how ideas **travel**, take form, and **transform**.

- A single YouTube video can build more rapport than 10 meetings.
- A powerful essay can shift public discourse.
- A personal story, vulnerably shared, can build a lifelong connection.

Real Example:

Brené Brown was an unknown researcher before her TEDx talk on vulnerability went viral. That **one piece of content** turned into a best-selling book empire, Netflix specials, and a cultural impact. She didn't sell a product. She gave language to people's **inner ache**. And the world responded.

3. Personal Reputation: The Silent Engine of Opportunity

In the idea economy, **you are the brand**.

Your **reputation** — what people feel when they hear your name — is your **most valuable asset**.

It moves **before you enter a room**, and works **long after you leave**.

Analogy:
Think of your reputation like a gravitational field. You don't

see it. But it **pulls or repels** people. It either opens or closes doors without you even knowing.

And the currency it builds is trust — the most scarce commodity of all.

Why This Is More Valuable Than Physical Assets

- **Ideas scale with zero marginal cost.** You don't need to own factories to impact millions.

- **Content lives forever.** A blog post from 2012 can still attract clients in 2025.

- **Reputation compounds.** One act of integrity in 2020 may bring a $10M opportunity in 2030.

Unlike physical assets — they cannot be stolen, inflated away, or eroded by rust or time.

Harry in the Modern World: The Digital Craftsman

Imagine Harry today.

He no longer hammers steel.

Instead, he writes. He shares truths. He teaches what he's lived.

- His **newsletter becomes a sanctuary** for those tired of surface-level advice.

- His **voice becomes a compass** for those lost in a noisy world.

- His **integrity becomes his brand** — and soon, he earns not just money, but **movement**.

Harry doesn't own factories. He doesn't sell products. But his **ideas**, his **voice**, and his **name** carry more weight than any warehouse full of goods.

That is **modern wealth**.

How You Can Start Today:

1. **Speak your truth — publicly.** Start a blog, podcast, or journal. Express what you know, love, and live.

2. **Nurture your reputation like a sacred flame.** Every word, every choice — leave behind trust, not just impressions.

3. **Document your journey.** Let others witness your growth. That vulnerability becomes your magnetism.

4. **Trade knowledge, not just time.** Package your insights into courses, books, and ideas that live beyond you.

5. **Stay consistent.** Value in this world builds quietly — but then it **explodes exponentially**.

Final Reflection:

"In the marketplace of today, ideas are the new iron, stories are the new steel, and your soul is the only forge that matters."

Let others chase buildings and balance sheets.

You? Build **presence, perspective,** and **principle**.

The wealth you'll generate will not just fill your account — it will **echo in eternity**.

Turning Inner Gold into Outer Wealth: The Alchemy of Monetising Wisdom

Arup sat by the river that once fed his childhood village. The water was still, but beneath its glassy surface, a thousand currents moved. He picked up a stone and turned it in his hand. Smooth. Polished. Weathered.

Just like him.

He thought back—not to his success, but to the years he carried ideas like unlit lanterns. Knowledge, yes. Creativity, yes. Skill, yes. But income? Freedom? Impact? They remained on distant shores.

Until he discovered something that changed everything:

"Wisdom alone does not liberate. It must be **shaped, shared**, and **systemised**."

This is the story of how Arup—and countless others—transformed what they *knew* into what they *earned*.

1. Codify the Invisible: From Intuition to Framework

Arup's first challenge was this: he knew *a lot*—but it lived in fragments. Insights scattered in journals, experiences buried in memory, lessons told in stories.

So he began **codifying**.

He turned patterns into principles. He named what was unnamed. He created frameworks for decision-making, healing, leadership, and design. He didn't just *do*—he started teaching others *how*.

Wisdom becomes transferable when it becomes teachable.

If you can't teach it, you can't scale it. And if you can't scale it, it cannot serve the world beyond your hands.

2. Build Your First "Product of the Mind"

Arup's first income-generating asset was not a factory, not a shop, not a patent. It was a **course**.

It packaged ten years of personal growth, learning from failures, and small wins in grassroots leadership. It was raw but real. People resonated—not because he was polished, but because he was precise.

Whether it's a book, an online course, a coaching program, a podcast, or a membership:

You are one product away from income that doesn't depend on your time.

He launched it. Taught ten people. Refined it. Then taught fifty. Then hundreds.

3. Choose the Right Platform for Your Voice

Arup wasn't everywhere. He chose one platform and *owned* it.

He hosted monthly talks on a community platform, where ideas could spread without the noise of distraction. He later repurposed that content for podcasts, newsletters, and collaborations.

In a noisy world, **depth trumps breadth.**

Find the one platform that honours your style. Write. Speak. Teach. Show. But don't just scatter—*root.*

4. Build a Value Ladder, Not Just a Product

After his first course, Arup offered deeper mentorship. Then a retreat. Then an inner circle.

Each level of offering provided **more transformation**, not just more information.

He wasn't selling content. He was selling **clarity, courage, and change.**

The wealthiest creators today don't just inform—they *transform.*
And transformation has levels. Price each according to the *value created*, not the time spent.

5. Automate and Delegate to Buy Time, Not Just Income

As Arup's model grew, he realised he was at risk of returning to the trap he left—**being busy again.**

So he documented every process. Automated emails, onboarding, and follow-ups. Delegated tasks he didn't love—design, admin, logistics—to freelancers who *did.*

The shift from **creator to asset builder** happens when your systems earn for you *even when you rest.*

6. Protect the Golden Source—Your Mind and Energy

Burnout is the death of creative income.

Arup created "sacred hours"—non-negotiable time for reading, reflection, and thinking. He learned:

Your next breakthrough will not come from hustle. It will come from silence.

He wasn't just building products. He was building **space** to listen, distil, and imagine.

The Parable of the Lampmaker

In an old town lived Elias, a lampmaker who was known across lands. People came for his lamps, yes—but more for the *light* they gave.

One day, a boy asked him, "What's the secret?"

Elias smiled. "The lamp is not the business. The flame is."

"You mean the light?"

"No. The **way to share light without burning out.** That's the real business."

Takeaway: Practical Steps to Monetise Wisdom

1. **Extract what you know** – turn it into frameworks, methods, or metaphors.

2. **Choose your delivery** – book, course, talk, service, or platform.

3. **Package your insight** – simple, valuable, and emotionally resonant.

4. **Deliver transformation** – not just information. Focus on *outcomes*.

5. **Create a system** – automate the repeatable. Delegate the drain.

6. **Expand wisely** – through partnerships, communities, and licensing.

7. **Protect your source** – rest, reflect, refill the creative well.

8. **Keep refining** – your first asset won't be perfect. But iterate with love.

The Bigger Truth

Money flows to **clarity**, **usefulness**, and **soul**.

Your knowledge becomes wealth when it solves *real pain* with *real grace*.

So ask not, "How can I make money?"

Ask:

"How can I serve at scale, from my soul—and sustain that service without breaking?"

That question will build a life and a legacy.

Just like Arup did—one light at a time.

The Wisdom-to-Wealth Framework

Turning Inner Brilliance into Sustainable Income & Impact

1. Illuminate → Clarify What You Know

"You can't monetise what you haven't defined."

- **Audit** your knowledge, life experiences, and talents.
- Identify recurring **patterns**, **insights**, and **frameworks**.
- Ask: *What do people often seek my help for?*

Tool: Mind Map or Personal Value Inventory

2. Distil → Create Transferable Frameworks

"Make the invisible visible. Make the intuitive teachable."

- Break your skills into teachable **steps, systems, or models**.
- Turn lived experience into **principles, metaphors, and stories**.
- Clarify *how* your process gets results.

Tool: 3-Step Signature Framework, Value-Transformation Map

3. Design → Build Your First Digital Asset

"Package your wisdom into something someone can hold, watch, read, or experience."

- Choose your **format**: eBook, course, coaching offer, workshop, template, or podcast.
- Focus on one **Minimum Viable Offering (MVO)**.
- Don't aim for perfect—aim for powerful and personal.

Tool: One Page Offer Canvas

4. Deliver → Solve Real Problems with Real Outcomes

"People pay for transformation, not just information."

- Position your asset with clear **benefits and results**.
- Serve a **niche pain point** or desire for clarity and empathy.
- Build trust through testimonials, results, and authentic storytelling.

Tool: Before–After–Bridge Copywriting

5. Systemise → Let Systems Do the Heavy Lifting

"Sustainable wealth is built by systems, not constant effort."

- Automate delivery: emails, onboarding, checkouts.
- Use platforms that scale (Teachable, Substack, Gumroad, Kajabi, Notion, etc.).

- Delegate what drains you. Focus on your **Zone of Genius**.

Tool: SOPs (Standard Operating Procedures), Tech Stack Map

6. Scale → Expand Without Losing Soul

"When your model works small, make it work wide."

- Add levels: free > core offer > premium offer > community.
- Repurpose content into books, talks, newsletters, or licensing models.
- Explore partnerships, affiliates, or group programs.

Tool: Value Ladder Blueprint

7. Sustain → Protect the Source (Yourself)

"The asset is not the product. It's you—you-your clarity, soul, and energy."

- Create sacred creative hours for deep work.
- Practice reflection, renewal, and realignment.
- Revisit your "why" quarterly—not just your revenue.

Tool: Personal Energy Calendar, Creative Sabbath Strategy

8. Legacy → Align Wealth with Meaning

"Make your assets echo through time."

- Invest profits into **long-term impact vehicles**—education, scholarships, content libraries, or social causes.

- Document and teach your process to others.

- Think in **decades**, not launches.

Tool: 10-Year Legacy Vision Map

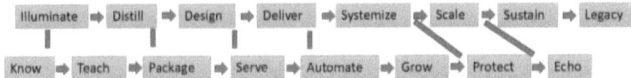

The Whisper That Becomes the Wind

How to Scale Without Burnout, Dilution, or Death of the Message

Arup sat alone in a room once filled with people—students, seekers, collaborators, believers. The bookshelves behind him held the journals he had written in for two decades, each filled with insights that once came as whispers in moments of quiet genius.

But now, he felt something deeper pulling at him—a sense that what he knew must live on, but not merely *through him*. The whisper had to become wind. It had to move *beyond* him.

He didn't want fame. He didn't even want followers.

He wanted the work to *breathe* without his breath.

To *move* without his constant motion.

To *teach* without his voice.

To *touch* without his hand.

From Expression to Expansion Without Exhaustion

Scaling what you know doesn't mean multiplying noise. It means *amplifying the essence*.

But most burn out because they try to clone themselves, not *extend* themselves.

The goal isn't to produce more of *you*, but to distil what is *true* in you into repeatable, resonant forms—**systems, stories, structures**, and **symbols**.

Imagine the difference between:

- A **flame** that burns endlessly only when you're near it.
- And a **lantern** that keeps glowing, long after you've stepped away.

The Emotional Trap of Scaling

People dilute their message when they start optimising for speed, trend, or validation.

They abandon what made them *sacred* in the first place:

- The lived truth.
- The crafted nuance.
- The patience of the process.

Why? Because the world rewards visibility more than *vitality*.

But wisdom that scales is *not louder*, it is *clearer*.

The Parable of the Seed and the Orchard

A seed holds within it the code of an entire forest.

But it doesn't shout.

It roots.

It waits.

It grows in stillness before it multiplies in silence.

Scaling wisdom is not about replication—it is about **germination**.

Your message, if planted right, will become an **orchard**, not a factory.

Practical Pillars for Scaling Without Dilution or Burnout

1. Codify the Core

Your message must be teachable, transferable, and timeless.

- What are your 3 guiding principles?
- What truth is non-negotiable, even if trends change?

Example: Arup turned his insights into a "Living Manifesto"—a 10-page sacred text that any reader could return to, interpret, and teach.

2. Systematise with Soul

Build **systems** that repeat the **spirit**, not just the script.

- Templates, frameworks, courses, books, protocols.
- Tools that guide people without needing your hand.

Example: Arup created interactive wisdom journals and audio meditations. His voice carried, but didn't carry the whole burden.

3. Mentor Multipliers

Don't teach followers—grow **custodians of the message**.

- Train a small group deeply.
- Let them evolve the message with integrity, not mimicry.

Example: Arup hand-picked 5 stewards. He didn't give them instructions—he gave them *questions* that once transformed him.

4. Let Go to Let Grow

Legacy begins when ego ends.

- Know when to step back, and let the work breathe.
- Trust that the wind will carry what the soul once whispered.

Example: Arup turned down a big platform deal because it wanted to change the tone of his story. He chose *continuity* over *clout*.

From Brilliance to Legacy

Real leverage is **not** about reaching millions. It's about building something that can **reach one, a million times**—without you having to perform endlessly.

Legacy isn't what you leave *behind*—it's what you build *beyond*.

Thought:

"What if your life's deepest work wasn't meant to be viral, but vital? Not fast-spreading, but long-lasting?"

Let your flame become fire.

Let your truth become a trail.

Let your voice become an echo.

Let it live, not just because *you* are here…

But because *it always was meant to be.*

The Wealth No One Sees

Why Invisible Capital Shapes the World—and How to Build It With Grace

The Story of Elias and the Empty Room

In a quiet corner of a fading city stood an old hall with peeling walls and dust-laced windows. Inside, a man named Elias spoke every Saturday—not to crowds, not to cameras, but to a circle of ten. Sometimes fewer. He wasn't famous. No banners. No books.

But one evening, after years of these small, sacred gatherings, a man named Jonah—a writer, broken by a world that had devoured his words and left him hollow—stumbled into that hall.

Elias said only one sentence that night.

"The truth doesn't need to be sold. It just needs to be held long enough for someone desperate enough to come looking."

Jonah never forgot it. He wrote again. But differently. Years later, when Jonah became a bestselling author, he told the world, *"My life was changed by a man who didn't even try."*

That is **invisible capital**.

What Is Invisible Capital?

It is **what can't be bought** but moves mountains. It's the compound wealth of:

- **Trust** (people believe you without needing proof)
- **Credibility** (your presence speaks louder than your pitch)
- **Thought leadership** (you don't chase attention; attention finds you)

It is built in whispers, but it *echoes* in the halls of time.

The Tree and the Shadow

Think of a giant banyan tree. Its shadow offers shelter, but the shadow can't exist without deep roots and a steady trunk.

- The **shadow** is your reputation, your visibility.
- The **trunk** is your credibility.
- The **roots** are trust, unseen but essential.
- The **soil**? That's character—what you do when no one sees.

Without roots, no shadow lasts.

Without a trunk, no leaves grow.

Why This Capital Is Often Overlooked

Because it's not immediate.

It doesn't spike followers.

It doesn't trend.

In a world chasing metrics, invisible capital is **measured in memory, not likes**.

It's why some voices fade after a viral post, while others echo long after they're gone.

We mistake visibility for influence. But true influence is when people carry your voice in their choices—without even realising it.

How to Consciously Cultivate Invisible Capital

1. Live in Alignment, Not Performance

Credibility is a *long game*.

When your private truth mirrors your public voice, trust takes root without announcement.

"Be the same person when the mic is off and the door is closed."

2. Build Depth Before Reach

Thought leadership is not volume. It's *clarity*.

- Say what others won't.
- Say what others feel but can't express.
- Say it with patience, not panic.

Example: Elias never asked for an audience. He became one with his message. And the world eventually leaned in.

3. Let Others Speak Your Name

Influence isn't what you say about yourself.

It's how others speak of you when you're not in the room.

- Serve in silence.
- Deliver when it matters.
- Let consistency become your brand.

4. Create Legacy-Driven Work

Do work that won't just be shared—it will be *returned to*.

- Books.
- Frameworks.
- Principles.
- Personal stories.

Give people tools they'll still be using 10 years from now.

Invisible Capital in Action:

- **Nelson Mandela:** Decades of silent resilience became a moral force that shaped nations.
- **Fred Rogers (Mr. Rogers):** Quiet empathy became multigenerational trust.
- **Your grandmother's hands:** May never have written a book, but shaped your entire moral compass.

Invisible Capital vs Visible Noise

Aspect	Invisible Capital	Visible Metrics
Time to build	Slow (years, decades)	Fast (days, months)
Source	Integrity, insight	Tactics, timing
Impact	Deep and long-term	Wide but often shallow
Carried by	Memory and transformation	Algorithms and trends
Reward	Influence, trust, legacy	Popularity, applause

Thought:

"What you build in silence today becomes the voice of trust tomorrow."

You don't have to scream to be heard.

You don't have to sell to be remembered.

You don't have to chase to lead.

Build your invisible capital.

Let your integrity do the marketing.

Let your clarity do the scaling.

Let your truth do the talking.

And remember: **The wealth that cannot be seen is often the only wealth that lasts.**

THE INVISIBLE CAPITAL TREE

"What grows in silence shapes the forest."

ROOTS – TRUST *(Unseen, but foundational)*

- Built through integrity, reliability, and emotional safety.
- Grown over the years, often without reward.
- Without roots, nothing sustains.

"Trust isn't built when you're right, but when you're consistent."

Practices:

- Keep small promises (to others and yourself).
- Show up when it's inconvenient.
- Speak less, listen more.

TRUNK – CREDIBILITY *(The stable spine of your presence)*

- Created by delivering value over time.
- It is your lived experience, not your résumé.
- Holds up everything else.

"Credibility is the echo of your actions over time."

Practices:

- Be the same person onstage and off.
- Publish work that withstands scrutiny.
- Let your mistakes inform your wisdom, not tarnish it.

BRANCHES – THOUGHT LEADERSHIP

- The unique perspective you bring to the conversation.
- Not just knowledge—but wisdom with voice and direction.
- Branches grow slowly, but once formed, they shape the canopy.

"You don't need to know everything. Just say what only you can say."

Practices:

- Write, speak, and share ideas with honesty and clarity.
- Stand for something—not everything.
- Let your silence be strategic, not timid.

FRUITS – REPUTATION & LEGACY *(What others carry forward)*

- You don't control the fruit—you cultivate the conditions.
- When roots and trunk are strong, fruit comes naturally.
- It feeds others, long after you've left.

"Legacy is not what you build for yourself, but what others build because of you."

Practices:

- Teach what you've lived.
- Mentor someone quietly.
- Build work that survives you.

The Invisible Capital Compass:

Compass Point	Invisible Resource	Guiding Question
North	Integrity (Root)	*"Am I aligned when no one is watching?"*
East	Wisdom (Branch)	*"What truth am I here to express uniquely?"*
South	Legacy (Fruit)	*"What seeds am I planting for others?"*
West	Presence (Trunk)	*"Is my voice anchored in lived truth?"*

Cycle of Invisible Capital

1. **Practice silence before opinion.**
2. **Serve value before asking for attention.**
3. **Stay consistent in obscurity.**
4. **Let others carry your truth forward.**

The Iceberg of Influence

"Invisible capital is like an iceberg. What the world sees is only the tip: your success, your voice, your influence. But the mass beneath—trust, character, discipline, credibility—is what keeps it afloat. Without it, even brilliance will drift and dissolve."

So keep building. Quietly. Deeply. Faithfully.

Because when storms come—and they always do—only the rooted remain.

CHAPTER III

The Energetics of Wealth

"Real wealth doesn't chase—it calls. It's not a hunt, but a hum."

— Shree Shambav

Synopsis

The Energetics of Wealth invites readers into a deeper layer of prosperity—beyond strategies and systems—into the field of vibration, magnetism, and alignment. This section decodes the often overlooked truth: money flows where energy aligns. Rather than chasing wealth, we learn to embody the frequency of it. By working with the subtle body, clearing energetic blockages, and becoming receptive rather than resistant, one opens the gateway to abundance that feels natural and fulfilling. The key isn't always action—it's energetic congruence. Wealth begins to arrive when you stop reaching and start resonating.

The Resonance of Riches: How Your Frequency Shapes Your Fortune

The Hidden Tuning Fork of Wealth

In an old village tucked away in the highlands, there was a story passed down through generations. It spoke of a man named Elior who lived in a modest hut on the edge of the valley. He had no land, no inheritance, and no formal education. Yet, strangely, wealth came to him—opportunities, allies, and prosperity followed him like loyal birds.

When the villagers asked his secret, he only smiled and said, "I keep my instrument in tune."

People laughed. Some dismissed it as a metaphor, others thought he was mad. But those who observed closely noticed something: Elior gave more than he took, he spoke with warmth, listened with presence, and even in the harshest winters, he wore a peace on his face that looked like summer.

Years later, a travelling mystic came to the village and heard of Elior. When she met him, she simply bowed. "You live as a tuning fork," she said. "And life cannot help but harmonise around you."

The Vibration of Wealth: A Deeper Truth

Wealth is not just material. It is a form of energy—one that responds, reflects, and resonates. Your *personal vibration*—your emotional tone, mental clarity, and energetic alignment—is the magnet behind the money.

The universe, like a vast sound chamber, responds to frequency. When you operate from fear, scarcity, resentment, or guilt, you emit a low vibration. These frequencies don't repel money by law, but by resonance—they attract what matches them: struggle, anxiety, short-term gain followed by long-term loss.

Conversely, when you elevate your vibration—through joy, integrity, trust, creativity, and gratitude—you become a frequency match for abundance. Money begins to flow, not because of luck or hustle, but because you're now aligned with *receiving*, not just desiring.

A Radio Dial and Static

Imagine your life as a radio, and wealth as a broadcast frequency. If your inner dial is tuned to static (fear, doubt, unworthiness), you won't receive the wealth channel clearly—even if it's broadcasting all around you.

But if you fine-tune your dial—through stillness, intentionality, gratitude, aligned action—you start to receive wealth with clarity and strength. It's not magic. It's resonance.

Arup's Awakening:

Arup, at one point, had all the right qualifications, the network, and the hustle. Yet, he was broke—emotionally and financially. He constantly felt like he was chasing something elusive. The more he ran toward money, the more it ran away from him.

One evening, after yet another failed pitch, he found himself sitting at the base of an old banyan tree in silence. An old sage who was watching him said, "You are chasing a river upstream. But rivers flow to those who prepare the land."

That moment shattered something in Arup. He stopped "hunting money" and started healing himself. He invested in his inner world—his beliefs, self-talk, sleep, and emotional regulation. He practised gratitude every morning, not as a routine, but as a conversation with life. Slowly, opportunities came—not massive, but frequent. His clients stayed longer, paid more, and referred others. His work deepened. His wealth expanded. And most of all, his *peace* grew richer than his bank account.

Practical Ways to Raise Your Frequency

1. **Audit Your Emotional Baseline**

   Track your most frequent emotions over a week. Are they rooted in fear, control, or joy? Awareness is step one.

2. **Elevate Through Environment**

   Surround yourself with spaces, people, and content that expand you. Your outer world reflects and reinforces your inner frequency.

3. **Practice Gratitude Energetically**

   Not just journaling—but feeling gratitude in your body. Let it vibrate. This anchors you in abundance.

4. **Release Scarcity Anchors**

   Forgive old financial wounds. Stop speaking about money with bitterness. Let go of the "never enough" narrative.

5. **Create from Overflow, Not Desperation**

   Don't build out of fear. Let your work be a song of service. Money comes when value is felt, not forced.

6. **Silence = Frequency Reset**

Spend time daily in silence. When you quiet the noise, your natural frequency returns. And it's often higher than you think.

7. **Affirm and Act in Alignment**

   Say it, believe it, live it. "I am a worthy steward of wealth." Then follow it up by acting like one.

Money is an Echo

Wealth doesn't begin in the wallet. It begins in your vibration. The outer world is the echo of your inner song. If you want the world to respond differently, sing a different note.

Let your actions hum with clarity. Let your thoughts rise like sacred music. Let your emotions anchor into joy.

And like Elior, you won't need to chase money.

You'll become the place it chooses to arrive.

Magnetism vs. Force: The Soul's Currency in the Dance of Wealth

The Parable of Two Gardeners

Once, in a quiet valley between two hills, lived two gardeners—**Lucas** and **Sophia**. Both dreamed of creating the most beautiful garden, a place where nature and prosperity could bloom in harmony.

Lucas began with force. He ploughed the earth with urgency, pulled roots aggressively, and forced seeds into the soil. He would shout at the rain, beg the sun, and spend sleepless nights battling weeds. His garden grew, but it was patchy—often dry, occasionally flooded, and strangely lifeless despite his constant effort.

Sophia, on the other hand, began with stillness. She sat with the land first. Observed the direction of the wind, the language of the soil, and the rhythm of the birds. She chose her seeds carefully, watered gently, tended to weeds daily but patiently. She didn't chase results—she tuned into the cycles. Her garden took longer, but it flourished—abundant, lush, humming with bees and peace.

One day, Lucas visited her garden, and with tears in his eyes, said, "I worked harder than you did—why does your garden feel like heaven, and mine like exhaustion?"

Sophia smiled softly, "Because you chased life. I listened to it."

Force vs. Magnetism: The Core Distinction

Force says: *"I must do more. I must prove. I must hustle, grind, push, compete."*

It's built on the architecture of fear—fear of not enough, fear of being left behind, fear of failure. Force is loud, tense, and often misaligned. It leads to temporary wins and deep internal erosion.

Magnetism whispers: *"I align. I attract. I become the kind of person who receives."*

It's rooted in presence, clarity, self-trust, and integrity. Magnetism doesn't mean passivity—it means **intentionality**. It means you move not to chase, but to express.

When you operate through magnetism, people feel your depth. Opportunities find you. Wealth gravitates because **value flows from you effortlessly**—like a river from the hills.

The Energetic Truth: Chasing Pushes Things Away

Think of trying to catch a butterfly.

Chase it, and it flutters just out of reach.

Stand still, wear flowers, and breathe in peace—and it may land on your shoulder.

The same is true for wealth, love, and opportunity. When you **chase**, your energy says, *I don't have it*. The frequency of lack repels. But when you **align**, your energy says, *I am already enough*—and like the butterfly, abundance is drawn in.

Arup's Inner Shift: A Story of Magnetism

Arup, once again, stood at a threshold. His previous years were spent mastering the art of execution—he built things, fixed things, solved things. But he noticed something: The more he hustled for money, the more burned out he became. The clients he attracted were needy. The results always seemed just out of reach.

Then, a quiet voice inside asked him:

"What if it's not about doing more—but being more?"

So he began a new journey—not outward, but inward.

He cleaned his inner space. Rewrote the stories of scarcity taught to him as a child. Stopped taking clients who felt wrong, even if they paid well. He created from joy, not fear. He wrote content from his soul, not just strategy. Slowly, people began to reach out. Invitations came in. One client said, "I don't even know what service you offer—but your presence feels grounded. I want that."

Arup realised: *Force got him noticed. Magnetism made him unforgettable.*

Practical Path: Cultivating Magnetic Wealth

1. **Heal the Scarcity Narrative**

    Ask yourself: What belief am I acting from—trust or lack? Replace fear-based beliefs with grounded truths: "I am safe. I offer value. I allow wealth."

2. **Align Identity with Outcome**

    Don't try to get wealthy—become the kind of person wealth naturally moves toward. Who do you need to be for that life?

3. **Create from Overflow, Not Need**

    Pour your gifts from fullness. People can feel the difference between creation born of desperation and that born of joy.

4. **Hold Vision, Release Control**

   Desire without clinging. Act without attachment. Let your vision be your North Star, not your prison.

5. **Strengthen Energetic Hygiene**

   Your mind, body, and environment are frequency tools. Clean them daily. Your vibration precedes your voice.

6. **Say No to Misalignment**

   Every "yes" to the wrong client, project, or path lowers your signal. Magnetism requires purity of direction.

7. **Rest as Strategy**

   Stillness is not the absence of productivity—it is the womb of clarity. Rest magnetises clarity. Clarity attracts aligned action.

Wealth Is a Mirror

If you're striving constantly but feel empty, check your **signal**, not your schedule.

Wealth doesn't come to the loudest.

It comes to the clearest.

Not to the chasers, but to the **calmest beacons of value.**

Build yourself into a cathedral of resonance. Let your life hum with alignment. And you'll see—what you once begged for, you now draw in with grace.

The Dam in the River: How Energy Blocks Repel the Flow of Wealth

"Abundance is not something you earn. It's something you remember how to allow."

The Story of the Silent Inheritance

In a quiet corner of the Himalayan foothills, Arup sat cross-legged inside a dimly lit stone hut—his journal open, but blank. It had been three weeks since he left the chaotic rhythm of city life. He had arrived in this retreat not to find wealth, but to understand why—despite years of effort, knowledge, discipline, and self-work—his life felt... stuck.

He'd built businesses. Earned enough. Lost some. Rebuilt. And yet, abundance always felt like something that visited but never stayed. Like a guest who dines at your table and vanishes before dawn.

That morning, an old monk named Rinpoche approached him with a question.

"If a river cannot reach the sea, do you blame the sky for not raining enough, or do you check if something is blocking its flow?"

Arup's eyes softened. Something in that sentence cracked open the silence within him.

"Let's walk," Rinpoche said, and led Arup to a mountain stream. But unlike the usual flowing waters, this one was still—trapped behind a natural barricade of stones and fallen branches.

"This stream should reach the valley below. It doesn't, because long ago, debris settled here, one by one. A storm, a fallen tree, and time... built a dam."

"Just like that," he continued, "your emotional wounds, unprocessed guilt, shame, fear, and scarcity... they build dams inside your energy field. You do everything right externally—but your inner river is blocked."

The Invisible Walls We Build

We often believe wealth is about effort, strategy, and intelligence. And while those are helpful, they are not the root.

Wealth is energy. It is flow.

When that flow is blocked—whether by fear of being seen, guilt over past mistakes, beliefs that money corrupts, or the unconscious programming inherited from generations of financial struggle—we cannot receive, let alone hold, abundance.

Here are some **common energy blocks**:

- **Emotional:**
    - Shame over past failures.
    - Fear of being perceived as greedy.
    - Guilt around "having more" than others.
- **Mental:**
    - Beliefs like "I must work hard to deserve money."

- "I'm not the kind of person who becomes wealthy."
- "If I get rich, people will abandon or resent me."

- **Spiritual:**
    - Internal split between material success and spiritual purity.
    - Subconscious vows of poverty or rejection of the physical world.
    - Belief that suffering is more noble than thriving.

These blocks operate **beneath the surface**—like the rocks under the river. You don't see them. But you feel them in the recurring patterns:

- You earn money but can't keep it.
- You get close to success, then sabotage.
- You attract wealth but feel guilty receiving it.

The Broken Vessel

Imagine trying to collect rain in a cracked pot. No matter how much water falls from the sky, it slowly leaks through invisible fractures. You don't need more rain—you need to seal the vessel.

Your body, your nervous system, your beliefs—they are the vessel.

Until you heal the inner fractures, more money, opportunities, or luck won't fix the feeling of "not enough."

Healing Moment

Later that evening, Arup sat by the fire and wrote the following words:

"I forgive myself for believing that I must suffer to be worthy. I release the shame of generations that taught me lack was safer than plenty. I now choose to receive—not as a beggar at the gates, but as a child returning home."

And with that, a new current stirred in him. Not fireworks. Just a subtle shift—a lightness. The beginning of flow.

Steps to Unblock Your Wealth Energy

1. **Acknowledge the Dam**

    - Write down recurring money patterns that hurt.
    - Reflect: "Where do I feel unworthy of abundance?"

2. **Name the Block**

    - Is it guilt? Fear of being judged? Loyalty to family struggle?
    - Giving it a name robs it of power.

3. **Energetic Releasing Ritual (daily or weekly)**
    - Speak aloud or journal:

"I see you, Fear. You protected me before. But I no longer need you to block my flow."

4. **Somatic Practice**
    - Breathwork, EFT tapping, or movement to release stored tension.
    - Wealth isn't just mental—it must feel *safe* in the body.

5. **Visualise a Flowing River**
    - Picture your energy, ideas, and self-worth as water.
    - Ask daily: "Where have I built walls?" Then gently dismantle them.

Reflection

Abundance doesn't arrive when you finish striving.

It arrives when you stop hiding.

You do not need to chase wealth.

You need to **clear the inner path** so that what's already destined for you can reach you.

When Arup returned from the mountains months later, nothing had changed in the world outside.

But *he* had.

And because of that, everything began to flow.

Journal Prompts & Exercises:

1. "What emotions do I carry about wealth that may be blocking me?"
2. "What did my parents or culture teach me—directly or indirectly—about money?"
3. "Do I believe I must earn love, comfort, or rest? Why?"
4. *Energetic Inventory:* Scan your body. Where do you hold tightness when thinking about money?
5. Practice *Wealth Affirmations* daily:
    - "It is safe for me to receive."
    - "I trust the flow of life and abundance."
    - "Wealth is my birthright, not my burden."

The Currency of the Subtle Body: How Chakras, Breath & Presence Align with Abundance"

"When your inner currents are blocked, no outer wealth can ever satisfy you. But when energy flows within, even silence feels rich."

The Story: Amar and the Merchant of Winds

In the ancient desert town of Zeyara—where the winds carried stories older than kings—Amar wandered, searching not for gold, but for peace.

He had come far in his material pursuits: his ventures were stable, his name respected, his shelves full of accolades. Yet inside, something felt hollow—like a golden chalice with no wine.

One day, a traveller told him of an old wind merchant who lived in the hills. "He doesn't sell wares," the man warned. "He sells insight—but only to those brave enough to inhale the winds of their own soul."

Intrigued, Amar climbed the winding paths and found the old merchant meditating among wind chimes. The man didn't ask Amar what he wanted. Instead, he offered him a simple instruction:

"Sit. Breathe. Feel where your breath refuses to go."

At first, Amar scoffed. He had met financial planners, therapists, and strategists. But a man who taught breath?

Still, he obeyed.

And within moments, he found it: tightness in his chest. A tension in his belly. A constriction in his throat. His breath—his very life force—wasn't flowing freely. Something was blocked.

The merchant spoke softly.

"You see, wealth is not earned from the world—it's magnetised from within. Your breath tells me your energy centres are tangled. Until your subtle body flows, you will build empires that cannot hold you."

The Map Within: Subtle Body and Money Flow

In the ancient traditions of yoga, tantra, and many indigenous spiritual systems, the **subtle body**—comprising **chakras, nadis (energy channels), prana (life force), and breath**— is the invisible architecture that determines how life flows through us.

When these systems are aligned, we don't just feel *spiritually whole*—we become powerful vessels for receiving, circulating, and anchoring wealth.

Let's explore **how each chakra**—when balanced or blocked—affects our **relationship with money and abundance**:

1. Root Chakra (Muladhara) – Security, Survival

When blocked:

Fear around money, hoarding, scarcity mindset, never feeling safe—even with enough.

When aligned:

Deep trust in life. Grounded financial decisions. A felt sense of "I am safe. I will always be supported."

Wealth, at its core, begins with safety. If you don't feel rooted, you'll chase money to calm anxiety, not to expand life.

2. Sacral Chakra (Svadhisthana) – Creativity, Flow

When blocked:

Shame around receiving. Repressed desires. Creativity stifled. Undervaluing your gifts.

When aligned:

Joyful creation. Pleasure in exchange. Openness to collaboration. Receiving becomes natural.

Money flows like water. If your inner rivers are dry, so will your outer streams be.

3. Solar Plexus Chakra (Manipura) – Power, Confidence

When blocked:

Imposter syndrome. Overworking to prove worth. Controlling behaviours. Resistance to delegation.

When aligned:

Healthy self-esteem. Leadership. Earning without burnout. Making clear financial boundaries.

Your ability to earn sustainably is tied to your belief that you deserve ease, not just effort.

4. Heart Chakra (Anahata) – Generosity, Connection

When blocked:

Fear of betrayal. Giving out of guilt. Transactional relationships. Attachment to money for validation.

When aligned:

Giving and receiving from wholeness. Integrity in business. Love-infused wealth decisions.

Abundance without love is noise. Abundance with love is music.

5. Throat Chakra (Vishuddha) – Expression, Truth

When blocked:

Fear of charging fairly. Hiding your voice. Inauthentic branding. People-pleasing to get clients.

When aligned:

Speaking value clearly. Attracting wealth through truth. Building a trust-based reputation.

Your wealth is limited by what you're afraid to say out loud.

6. Third Eye Chakra (Ajna) – Vision, Intuition

When blocked:

Disconnected from purpose. Chasing trends. Confusion about direction. Second-guessing yourself.

When aligned:

Clear inner vision. Inspired business ideas. Bold, intuitive leaps. Inner knowing guides strategy.

The greatest wealth strategy is a vision that's soul-backed, not market-forced.

7. Crown Chakra (Sahasrara) – Spiritual Connection

When blocked:

Overattachment to material success. Cynicism. Disconnection from gratitude. Hustling without joy.

When aligned:

Trust in divine timing. Humble surrender. A wealth path that feels sacred. Freedom beyond numbers.

When you remember you are infinite, you no longer beg life for scraps.

The Human Bank of Light

Imagine each chakra as a vault in a seven-story bank. If one vault is rusted shut, wealth cannot move freely. Even if your top floors (vision, strategy) are strong, if the ground floor (safety, trust) is weak—the whole building trembles.

Your **breath** is the key. Your **presence** is the vault cleaner. Your **awareness** is the accountant. When they align, you become a **Human Bank of Light**—a soul whose balance sheet reads: *Rich in energy, rich in grace.*

Practical Steps: Bridging Inner Alignment with Outer Abundance

1. **Daily Chakra Check-In (5 mins)**

    Close your eyes. Breathe into each chakra. Ask: *"Am I open here?"* Notice sensations or blocks.

2. **Somatic Wealth Practice**

   Choose a wealth affirmation:
   - ○ "I am safe to receive."
   - ○ "My voice attracts abundance."
   - ○ "My presence magnetises value."

   Speak it while breathing deeply and gently placing your hands over the related chakra.

3. **Breath as Currency**

   Practice box breathing (4-4-4-4) or alternate nostril breathing to cleanse energy and centre the mind.

4. **Heart-Centred Earning**

   Before sending an invoice, proposal, or launching a product, place your hand on your heart and ask:

   "Does this reflect my love, truth, and integrity?"

5. **Spiritual Financial Planning**

   Map your wealth goals not only by numbers, but by **energy alignment**:
   - ○ Does this income source feel light or heavy?
   - ○ Am I choosing this path out of fear or flow?

Reflection: Amar's Whisper

That evening, back at the wind merchant's hut, Amar finally understood:

"Money is not the wind," the old man said. "You are the wind. Money is the echo it leaves when you move through the world with aligned breath."

And from that day on, Amar no longer chased windfalls. He simply cleared his channels, breathed fully—and let abundance flow where it naturally wanted to go.

Journal Prompts:

1. Which chakra do I feel most blocked in when it comes to money?

2. What breath or embodiment practice makes me feel most abundant—before a single rupee enters my account?

3. Where do I still equate spiritual purity with material lack?

4. What would it mean to let money flow *through* me, not *to* me?

PART TWO

INTEGRATION — Living a Life that Outlives You

"You don't leave a legacy by dying rich. You leave one by living richly."

-Shree Shambav

CHAPTER IV

Legacy that Outlives You

"Money can open doors. Character keeps them open for generations."

— Shree Shambav

Synopsis

Legacy that Outlives You explores the soul of lasting wealth—an impact that reverberates through generations. This section expands wealth from possession to purpose, revealing how true legacy is built not just in vaults or estates, but in the values we embody and the lives we elevate. By transitioning from self to service, we learn to use power and prosperity as instruments for the greater good. This is where influence becomes timeless—when your life becomes a bridge for others to rise, when your existence plants seeds for a future you may never see, yet always shaped.

From Spotlight to Lighthouse: The Alchemy of Selfless Success

"True success is not how brightly you shine, but how many lives your light guides home."

Arup and the Empty Palace

In the later years of his life, Arup had reached the summit of what most would call success. His ventures flourished, his investments multiplied like rain-fed seeds, and his name—once whispered with hope—was now declared with admiration.

But one day, walking through the great marble halls of his estate—his feet echoing across emptiness—he felt a strange hollowness.

He paused in front of a giant mirror. There stood a man dressed in elegance, surrounded by gold, but with a gaze that asked a question no wealth could answer:

"And then what?"

He had climbed the mountain of ambition. But now he wondered if he had built a throne... or a cage.

That evening, he visited an old school he once funded anonymously, tucked in the edge of a forgotten village. Children ran barefoot, laughing. A young girl stood on a broken bench and read a poem she had written—about dreams, and rivers, and flying.

Arup wept.

Not because the poem was perfect.

But because it was *alive*.

"This," he whispered to himself, "is the only return that matters. This is legacy—not what I own, but what I ignite."

From Success to Significance: A Deeper Shift

Many of us spend our early years building the architecture of success—accumulating wealth, mastery, influence. But if we stop there, it becomes a monument to self—a grand structure visited by applause, yet abandoned by the soul.

True wealth begins to transform when we ask:

- *Whom does this serve?*
- *What ripple am I creating beyond my name?*
- *What seed am I planting that may bloom long after I'm gone?*

This is the sacred shift—from **self-centred success to soul-centred service.**

The Spotlight and the Lighthouse

Imagine success as a **spotlight**. It shines brightly on the individual. It dazzles, commands attention, and draws applause.

But service is a **lighthouse**. It does not demand attention—it offers direction. It doesn't move—but it helps others find their way through storms.

The spotlight feeds the ego. The lighthouse feeds the world.

And strangely, in that offering, the soul feels nourished in a way no applause ever could.

Why This Shift Changes Everything

1. It Redefines Wealth

Instead of viewing money as a symbol of status, it becomes a **tool of empowerment**—a bridge between potential and impact.

A dollar given with purpose is worth more than a million hoarded with fear.

2. It Cultivates Enduring Influence

Influence built on service outlasts trends. When people feel *seen, helped, healed*, they remember—and they carry your legacy in their own actions.

Reputation is borrowed. Impact is immortal.

3. It Heals the Inner Hunger

Many chase success, hoping to silence inner wounds. But true healing begins when we turn outward—not to impress, but to uplift.

Service fills the cracks that achievement cannot reach.

The Three Levels of Legacy

Let's break this transformation into three layers:

1. Personal Legacy

Healing yourself, breaking generational patterns, and cultivating emotional and financial sovereignty.

This is the root.

Without this, service becomes martyrdom.

2. Interpersonal Legacy

How you treat your clients, team, family, and community. What values do you embody in everyday exchanges?

This is the branch.

Even a small act—like a kind message or fair deal—ripples.

3. Universal Legacy

The movements you support, the ideas you champion, the systems you build that serve beyond your lifetime.

This is the fruit.

When the work lives on without needing you.

How to Begin This Shift Practically

1. Anchor Your "Why"

Ask:

- If I had all the money I needed, *what would I build or contribute?*
- What change breaks my heart—and how could my work be part of its healing?

2. Audit Your Impact

Examine:

- Are my business and creative choices aligned with people's growth—or only profit?

- How does my service *feel* to those receiving it?

3. Serve Without Attachment

Give where you won't get a return.

Offer your time, insight, or presence without the demand for recognition.

Let your service be anonymous enough to be pure, and intentional enough to matter.

4. Build Platforms, Not Pedestals

Instead of being the centre, create ecosystems where others thrive.

Build:

- Scholarships, not just success stories.
- Tools, not just trophies.
- Processes that can run without your constant presence.

A Moment with Arup: The Returning Echo

Years after Arup's quiet transformation, he received a letter—handwritten—from that same girl who once read him her poem.

She had become a teacher, returned to her village, and now ran a small school.

At the bottom of the letter, she wrote:

"You didn't just build a school. You built me.

And now, I build others. Your legacy is walking, barefoot and brave."

And that night, Arup finally felt *rich*.

Journal Prompts for Reflection:

1. What would remain of your work if your name were erased?
2. Who benefits from your success today—beyond you?
3. What cause, community, or human story moves you enough to act?
4. What does "impact" look like in your world—not just income?

Thought:

Success is a milestone. Service is a movement.

The day you stop asking *"How much can I get?"*

And begin asking, *"How much can I give, grow, and guide?"*—

That is the day your wealth starts to whisper eternity.

The Seed or the Shadow: Redefining Wealth as Empowerment

"You can leave behind a vault or a vision. One preserves the past. The other empowers the future."

The Two Sons and the Orchard

In a quiet village nestled between two rivers, an elder named Daelen had spent a lifetime building his estate. He had orchards that bore fruit in every season, lands that whispered prosperity, and a vault filled with gold he had earned through decades of toil and trade.

As he approached the end of his life, he called his two sons—Rowan and Elias—and offered them a choice.

To Rowan, he said, "Take the vault. Every coin is yours. You may never need to work again."

To Elias, he said, "Take the orchard. Learn its seasons. Cultivate its soil. It may not give you instant riches—but it will feed you and many more, if you care for it."

Years passed.

Rowan lived lavishly. But without understanding value, the vault dwindled. His comfort bred dependence, not wisdom. When the gold ran dry, so did his direction.

Elias, on the other hand, became a master of the land. He learned when to prune, when to wait, and when to plant. His hands were calloused, but his heart was full. He not only fed his family—he taught others how to grow. Soon, villages around him bloomed too.

One inherited wealth.

The other inherited *the ability to generate it.*

Only one left a legacy.

The Myth of Monetary Inheritance

Many believe that passing on money is the ultimate act of love or responsibility. But *money alone is inert.* It has no guidance, no discipline, no wisdom without a steward. Like giving a ship without a compass, money given without a mindset creates confusion, not clarity.

Wealth is not just what you leave behind. It is what you embed within.

The question is not: *How much do I give them?*

It is: *What kind of person do they become with what I've given?*

Fire or Flame

Wealth is like **fire**. In the hands of the unprepared, it burns, blinds, and destroys. But in the hands of the wise, it warms homes, lights paths, and cooks sustenance.

You can give someone a roaring fire…

Or teach them to tend a flame.

A roaring fire may die in a night. A tended flame becomes a hearth for generations.

The Shift: From Inheritance to Empowerment

Inheritance says:

"Here is what I've accumulated for you."

Empowerment says:

"Here's how to become someone who can create, steward, and multiply this value with purpose."

Empowerment is harder. It takes patience. It demands that you:

- Share your **mistakes**, not just your victories.
- Expose your **beliefs**, not just your balance sheets.
- Model **integrity**, not just opulence.

But empowerment *lasts*. Inheritance, if unaligned with values, *fades*.

Arup's Lesson: The Quiet Fund

Years after his transformation, Arup began something most would never know.

He started what he called a "Quiet Fund" for his family. But it wasn't just money. It was filled with journals, voice notes, teachings, and letters.

Each grandchild would receive:

- A yearly **financial gift**
- A **life lesson**
- A **real-world challenge** (such as starting a mini-project, helping a cause, or mentoring someone else)

And they were only allowed to withdraw more if they showed how they were **growing—not just spending**.

His belief?

"I don't want to give them the river. I want to teach them to find the spring."

Five Ways to Turn Wealth into a Legacy

1. Model Mindsets, Not Just Mechanics

Let them see how you *think*—about risk, generosity, and purpose. Discuss your *philosophy* around money, not just tactics.

2. Build Learning Pathways

Create journals, videos, or "legacy letters." Teach through story, not lectures. Make your lessons emotionally rich and real.

3. Tie Wealth to Responsibility

Give in stages. Link gifts to growth. Foster stewardship, not dependence.

Wealth without responsibility leads to erosion. Wealth with responsibility leads to evolution.

4. Plant Generosity into the Framework

Encourage giving. Not from guilt, but from gratitude. Make philanthropy a family ritual.

Let them taste the joy of impact, not just the comfort of accumulation.

5. Invest in the Spirit, Not Just the System

Fund their healing. Support mentors, retreats, and inner work. A wounded soul will waste a fortune; a healed soul will multiply modest means into miracles.

Journal Prompts for Reflection:

1. What have I *learned* about money that I wish I knew earlier?

2. If I passed today, what *principles* around wealth would I want my children—or mentees—to carry forward?

3. What kind of stories, values, and scars have shaped my relationship with money?

4. How can I build a system that transmits *wisdom*, not just wealth?

Reflection:

True wealth is not how much you leave behind, but how well you prepared those who receive it.

You can give them the harvest.

Or you can teach them the rhythm of rain and roots.

One lasts a season.

The other—*a legacy*.

Beyond the Vault: The True Inheritance of Generational Elevation

"To elevate a generation, give them roots in wisdom and wings of vision. Gold without ground becomes dust; but values, if planted, bloom forever."

The Paradox of Wealth Transfer

Many families pass down money on love. But love alone, transmitted through assets, can't always withstand time.

We've seen it before—fortunes gained in one generation, lost in the next. Not because the heirs lacked access, but because they lacked *alignment*. What was missing wasn't money—but meaning.

Money may open doors, but only values determine what happens once you walk through them.

So the question becomes: *What lifts a generation?*

It's not inheritance.

It's **initiation**.

Not merely riches, but **rituals**—transmissions of *identity*, *insight*, and *inner discipline*.

The Story of Sienna and the Archive Room

Sienna grew up in a lineage known for real estate wealth. When her father passed, she inherited 12 properties—and one unexpected key.

It unlocked a dusty room in the old family house, filled with handwritten ledgers, letters, and recordings going back three generations.

Each ancestor had left behind:

- Reflections on choices they regretted.
- Philosophies about money and integrity.
- A list titled "What I Wish I Knew at 25."

The first note read:

"This house will age. The land will shift. But if you understand how we thought, you'll never be poor."

As Sienna poured through them, she realised the real estate wasn't the treasure. *The real inheritance was consciousness.*

She turned that room into what she called "The Living Archive." Every year, her children would enter it—*not to receive money, but to absorb memory.*

By the time they were ready to lead, they weren't just heirs—they were **embodied extensions** of a lineage grounded in soul and strategy.

What Must Be Passed On?

1. Foundational Values

The compass is behind every decision.

- **Integrity over impulse.**

- **Generosity with discernment.**
- **Gratitude as a wealth magnet.**
- **Humility as protection.**

Teach them to *value values* more than valuation.

2. Inner Systems of Clarity

It's not just about external systems (trusts, investments)—but *internal systems* of thinking.

- How to sit with doubt without acting from fear.
- How to delay gratification with purpose.
- How to listen to intuition over ego.

An inner compass prevents outer collapse.

3. Relational Wisdom

Wealth without relationship is emptiness in disguise.

Teach:

- How to resolve conflict with grace.
- How to navigate betrayal without bitterness.
- How to collaborate from alignment, not obligation.

Money may buy influence—but it's presence and empathy that build empires.

4. Spiritual Perspective

Anchor them in something beyond the material.

- Rituals of reflection.
- Moments of silence.
- Teachings on impermanence and surrender.

Let them know:

"You are not your wealth. You are the *vessel* through which wealth flows into the world."

5. Stories of Struggle and Spirit

Pass down *how you got here*, not just *what you got*.

"Here's how we survived bankruptcy."

"Here's when I almost lost it all—and what saved me."

"Here's why we give, even when it's uncomfortable."

Stories make values real.

Stories protect the wisdom behind the numbers.

6. Legacy Systems, Not Just Legal Structures

Yes—wills and trusts matter. But what about:

- **Legacy letters?**
- **Family forums** to debate, dream, and decide?
- **Mentorship circles** for the young to be guided?

Build living systems that outlast static documents.

The Framework: The 3 Tiers of Generational Elevation

Tier	What's Passed	Effect
Survival	Assets (money, property)	Temporary uplift
Stability	Systems (structures, strategies)	Sustained security
Elevation	Wisdom (values, practices, perspective)	Transcendent legacy

Most families stop at survival. Few rise to elevation.

But elevation is what turns inheritance into impact.

Exercises: Planting a Generational Garden

Write Your "Values Will"

List the top 5 values you want future generations to live by. Include a real story for each.

Create a Legacy Ritual

Choose a date (e.g., birthday, festival, anniversary) and create a ritual—storytelling, giving, journaling—that transmits wisdom.

Interview the Elders

Record conversations with elders in your family or community. Preserve the soulprint of their journey.

Design a Family Learning System

Books to read. Skills to develop. Causes to support. Let it evolve—but let it exist.

Share Your "Why" Behind Every Asset

For every property, investment, or gift, share the story behind it. Turn capital into consciousness.

Reflections:

"You are not just building wealth. You are building *a way of being* that will ripple through unseen tomorrows."

If you pass down gold without grounding, you've given them a storm.

But if you pass down *ethics, emotion, and elevation*—you've given them the stars.

Echoes in the Stillness: Designing a Life That Outlives You

"You will not be remembered by your possessions, but by what you possessed inside: the grace with which you walked, the courage with which you loved, and the silence you healed in others."

The Unspoken Architecture of Legacy

Legacy is often misunderstood.

People think it's the school named after them. The foundation was built in their honour. The children who carry their surname.

But legacy—true legacy—is much quieter.

It is the warmth someone feels when they repeat your words in a moment of darkness.

It is the courage someone draws when they remember how you stood your ground with grace.

It is the ripple you'll never see—but that pulses in the life of someone who never met you, yet felt you, through someone else.

You don't build that legacy by chasing remembrance.

You build it by choosing resonance—**every single day**.

Elias and the Garden with No Fence

Elias lived in a small village on the edge of an ever-shifting river. He was not the wealthiest man. Not the loudest. Few knew him beyond the hills.

But every morning, before sunrise, Elias watered his garden. Not just the plants within his property—but those that grew on the edges, where no one claimed the land.

Children used to ask, "Why is water where no one lives?"

Elias would smile, "One day, someone will."

Years passed. Elias passed. The river, wild as always, overflowed one year and swallowed many homes.

But the land Elias had tended—though unclaimed—remained lush, fertile, and safe. Families took shelter there. Seeds he planted bore fruit. His name became a prayer.

And no plaque marked his name.

But the earth remembered.

So did the people.

Designing an Echo: Three Dimensions of Enduring Impact

To design a life that echoes after you've left the room, the home, the body—consider these layers:

1. Spiritual Echo: Your Inner Resonance

This is not about religion.

It is about **who you are in silence**, when no one is watching.

- Do you live by your deepest truths?
- Do you return to your centre, even when it's hard?
- Is your presence a sanctuary or a storm?

"The soul's vibration does not die. It becomes part of the song others live by."

Design Practice:

Create daily rituals that connect you to stillness—meditation, walking barefoot, journaling in candlelight. Build your inner frequency like a tuning fork for others.

2. Emotional Echo: Your Impact on Intimacy

It's in the way you listen.

The way you hold a gaze without interrupting.

The way you offer dignity, especially to those who can do nothing for you.

- Do others feel safer after being with you?
- Did you give people space to feel like they mattered?

These moments don't make headlines, but they make **heart lines**—and those stretch far beyond death.

"To love deeply is to outlive your heartbeat."

Design Practice:

Each week, choose one relationship to nourish—not to fix, but to hold in love. A letter. A phone call. A moment of seeing. Let people know they're not invisible.

3. Social Echo: Your Contribution to the Collective

You don't need millions to create a movement.

You need **meaning** and the courage to plant it where others walk.

- Are your actions aligned with what the world deeply needs?
- Are you building systems, stories, or soil that will nourish beyond your time?

Arup began this through his writings, his teachings, and the way he mentored others—not by trying to be known, but by *knowing himself deeply and serving from that place.*

"Fame ends in a headline. Contribution echoes in humanity."

Design Practice:

Ask yourself monthly: *What will this action ripple into?*

Build with systems in mind: write your frameworks, record your lessons, mentor someone even when you're tired. What you build in alignment will be carried in silence.

A Tuning Fork in the Earth

Imagine placing a tuning fork in the soil. You strike it, and the vibration moves invisibly into the roots, the rocks, the hidden life below.

No one sees the vibration.

But when the wind passes through that same space a decade later, it sings in a certain tone—**yours**.

That's what it means to live in a way that leaves echoes.

Your vibration, your values, your vision—they are not forgotten.

They become *embedded in the landscape of the living.*

Reflection Prompts for Designing Your Echo

1. **The Final Letter**:

   Write a letter to the world 50 years after your death. What do you hope they remember—not about you, but about *how you made them feel and live?*

2. **Echo Inventory**:

   Write down 3 people whose lives you've touched in quiet ways. How? Why? What does it tell you about your essence?

3. **The Legacy Circle**:

   What practices, teachings, or creations of yours could become someone's ritual? Map out your top

4. **The Aligned Yes / Sacred No List**:

   What do you say YES to that is soul-aligned? What do you need to say NO to in order to stay in alignment with your echo?

Invocation

"Let me live so that the wind remembers me,

so that silence still carries my prayer,

and so that love—passing through a stranger's hands—

wears the shape of my offering."

This is how we become immortal.

Not by being remembered—

but by becoming part of how the world remembers *itself*.

CHAPTER V

Relationships and Social Capital

"The strongest connections are grown, not gathered."

Shree Shambav

Synopsis

Relationships and Social Capital explores the unspoken architecture of wealth—your human connections. In a world obsessed with net worth, this section reveals the priceless value of network worth. Trust, reputation, emotional reciprocity, and aligned networks form the bridges to influence, opportunities, and fulfilment. From strategic alliances to soul-level friendships, who you know—and how you show up in those connections—can either elevate or limit your rise. When built with intention, your relationships become a living reservoir of wisdom, support, and synergy, far more enduring than financial assets.

Guruji's words hung in the air, profound in their simplicity, yet vast in their implications. "Roopa," he said, his voice a blend of kindness and compassion, "minimalism goes far beyond the possessions we hold in our hands. It is a journey of the heart, the mind, and the soul. True minimalism touches every aspect of our lives—our relationships, our habits, our thoughts—and demands of us a sacred courage: the courage to let go of what does not serve us and to hold close what truly nourishes us."

The Currency of Connection: Why Who You Walk With Shapes Where You Arrive"

"Money can buy you a seat, but only trust invites you to the table."

The Illusion of Sole Currency

We live in a world where financial capital is worshipped as the master key—unlocking homes, cars, opportunities, and security.

And yes, money is powerful. It moves matter. It builds bridges and breaks barriers. But in the quiet corridors of enduring success and soul-deep fulfilment, **money alone is insufficient**.

Because money can open doors…

…but relationships open *realms*.

Because money may be spent to attract…

…but *trust is earned* to remain.

Arup and the Gatekeeper

Arup was once invited to speak at an international gathering—a chance to share his voice with the world. But there was a catch: he needed a special clearance, a sponsorship, something his finances alone couldn't provide.

He had the money. He could have pulled strings, made noise, pushed harder.

Instead, he made a quiet call to an elder friend, Meiling—a woman he had once helped during her difficult transition into a new country years ago. Back then, it had cost Arup time, empathy, and presence—not money.

Now, years later, her single call unlocked the gates.

"Not because you paid," she said, "but because years ago, *you paid attention.*"

The Two Vaults We Carry

Every person walks with **two invisible vaults**:

- One is filled with **money**—assets, accounts, and liquidity.
- The other holds **social capital**—trust, respect, connection, reputation, goodwill.

In times of crisis, one might drain your bank account.

But in moments of transition, transformation, or transcendence—it is your **social capital** that elevates you. It speaks when you're silent. It arrives before you do. It *vouches for your name when you're not in the room.*

The Ladder in the Forest

Imagine you are deep in a forest, surrounded by tall walls of opportunity. You can buy tools to climb—ropes, hammers, and ladders.

But someone who *knows the terrain*, who *has walked these woods before*, can simply point you to a hidden opening in the wall.

Social capital is that guide.

It doesn't always remove the work—but it **shortens the distance between you and destiny**.

Dimensions of Social Capital That Transcend Wealth

Let's explore how social capital quietly becomes a foundational force for lasting success:

1. Trust as Leverage

Financial capital gives access.

But *trust gives an invitation*.

Your consistency, integrity, and how you treat people—especially those who cannot offer you anything in return—become the silent resume that follows you.

Practice: Make deposits into the trust bank. Keep promises. Listen without an agenda. Speak truthfully, especially when it costs you comfort.

2. Reputation as Currency

Reputation isn't branding.

It's the *echo of your integrity* in rooms you've never entered.

Reputation can't be bought—it's *built* through your patterns, not performances.

Practice: Ask yourself weekly: "Would I be proud if my actions today were replayed by someone I love tomorrow?"

3. Relationships as Compounding Interest

Like compound interest, genuine relationships grow in value over time.

They offer referrals, reflections, collaborations, and, at times—redemption.

Make space for regular reconnection. Don't network. Nurture. Be generous in sharing others' work. Celebrate them publicly, support them privately.

4. Presence as Power

The world remembers how you made them feel more than what you gave.

Presence—your ability to be *fully there*—is a rare form of value in an age of distraction.

When in conversation, drop your agenda. Look people in the eye. Ask better questions. Speak less, hear more. Presence earns memory.

Legacy: What People Say When You Can No Longer Speak

In the end, the most powerful thing people say is not,

"He had millions,"

but
"He showed up."

"She believed in me."

"They made me feel seen when I was invisible."

That is social capital—**the wealth of heartprints.**

It weaves you into stories.

It lives inside others.

It doesn't need a bank.

It only needs *you*, present and true.

Reflection Questions: Designing a Relationship-Rich Life

1. **Who are your quiet gatekeepers?**

   Who in your life has been quietly watching, ready to support—but you haven't nurtured the relationship?

2. **How have you been investing in people?**

   Are you transactional or transformational?

3. **What do people feel when they think of your name?**

   Not just your resume. Your resonance.

4. **Are you living your eulogy or your elevator pitch?**

   Because one gets you a job. The other lives on.

An Insight

"The richest man in the village wasn't the one with the tallest gates,

but the one whose door had no lock—

and whose fire warmed the whole neighbourhood."

Build wealth. Yes.

But build **people** *as well.*

Because when storms come, it is not your money that will carry you.

It is the memory of your character, the fabric of your friendships,

and the bridges you built when you had no reason—

except love.

The Invisible Bridges: Trust, Value, and the Currency of Connection

"In a world chasing likes, the rarest form of wealth is still trust."

The Currency We Never Count

When people speak of "networking," they often picture business cards, handshakes, LinkedIn endorsements, or coffee meetings punctuated with polite ambitions. But underneath this outward motion lies a more sacred architecture—**a network built not on transaction, but transformation.**

These are not relationships formed in rushes of ambition, but in the **slow simmer of sincerity**.

They are sustained not by how much we know or even who we know—but **how deeply we are known and how generously we give.**

At the core of these lasting networks lie **three invisible currencies**:

- **Trust** (the spiritual glue)
- **Mutual value** (the shared ecosystem)
- **Emotional equity** (the soul investment)

Let's explore them through a story and unpack their practical, emotional, and spiritual significance.

Alex and the Vineyard Keeper

In a quiet hill town in northern Italy lived Alex, a young, driven entrepreneur hoping to start a wine export business. He had studied oenology, written business plans, and raised some funds.

But there was one obstacle—**he needed grapes**. Not just any grapes. He needed them from *Giovanni*, the most respected vineyard keeper in the region.

Giovanni, an old soul with weathered hands and sharper intuition, had received dozens of offers, all with money and promises.

Alex went to meet him.

He didn't pitch.

He didn't sell.

He *asked about the land.*

He listened to Giovanni speak of his soil like a sacred altar. Of the storms of '72 that nearly destroyed it. Of his wife, who used to sing while sorting grapes. Of how every vine had a name in her memory.

Alex didn't ask to buy. He asked to **learn**.

For months, Alex returned—helping harvest, listening to stories, and building a table for Giovanni's grandchildren.

One day, Giovanni handed Alex a crate of grapes with a single phrase:

"You've already earned them."

1. Trust: The Invisible Thread That Holds Everything Together

Trust is not declared. It is demonstrated.

It's not built through volume—but through **presence, consistency, and integrity**.

Trust means someone believes:

"You won't harm me when I'm vulnerable. You'll honour me when I'm not watching."

In both personal and professional networks, **trust is the gateway** to intimacy, collaboration, forgiveness, and shared growth.

Practice:

- Be *consistent* in word and deed, especially when no one is watching.

- Admit when you're wrong. That's where trust deepens.

- Don't overpromise. Underpromise and *overdeliver*.

2. Mutual Value: The Ecosystem, Not the Transaction

Strong networks are not one-way streets. They are **gardens**—interdependent, reciprocal, seasonal.

But value is not always material. It comes in many forms:

- Emotional safety
- Strategic insight
- Silent support during difficult seasons
- Opportunities that come not from favours, but *faith* in each other

A meaningful network asks:

"How can I be of value even when I'm not the centre of this conversation?"

Practice:

- Listen for what people *need*, not just what they *say*.
- Share ideas freely.
- Connect others without expecting anything in return.

Your unseen generosity becomes your unshakable reputation.

3. Emotional Equity: The Wealth of Shared Humanity

Emotional equity is what forms when you walk with someone *through* something:

- You held space for them when their father died.
- You believed in them before the world noticed.
- You forgave them when they faltered.
- You stayed, not because it was convenient, but because it was *true*.

This becomes a kind of sacred wealth—one that compounds silently over time.

People will forget your titles, your awards, your market cap.

But they will remember *how you held their name when it was fragile.*

Practice:

- Keep confidences.
- Celebrate others' wins as if they were your own.
- In moments of conflict, choose curiosity over condemnation.

The Bridge Over Invisible Rivers

Imagine every connection you build as a bridge over an invisible river.

Money might let you place a plank.

Power might add ropes.

But only **trust, mutual value, and emotional equity** can weather the storms that threaten to wash the bridge away.

The bridges we build in life—between hearts, between values, between generations—must be built from materials not sold in stores:

Presence. Integrity. Kindness. Courage. Listening. Giving without keeping score.

What Happens Without These Currencies?

- A vast network, but no one to call at midnight.
- A fat bank account, but no shared meals or soul laughter.
- Influence, but no intimacy.
- Visibility, but no one truly sees you.

This is the loneliness of hollow success.

What Happens When These Are Present?

- A call changes the course of your life.
- A quiet conversation becomes a turning point.
- A shared tear becomes a lifelong alliance.
- A reputation precedes you, not because of branding, but *because of being*.

This is the richness of a soul-connected life.

Reflection

"In the end, we are not remembered for our resumes,
but for the warmth in our tone,
the grace in our pauses,
and the way we made others feel like they mattered."

Journal Prompts for Application:

1. Who are three people you trust deeply—and why?
2. Where in your life can you give value without expectation?
3. How do you show up when someone else is struggling?
4. What kind of emotional equity have you built in the last year?

Circles of Fire or Fog: Finding Your Soul's Mirror in Others"

"You are not just choosing company—you are choosing your future echo."

The Hidden Architecture of Our Circles

Not all circles are created equal.

Some gather around **comfort**, others around **courage**.

Some are drawn to **familiarity**, others to **freedom**.

We rarely realise how much the **ecosystems of people** around us sculpt our beliefs, behaviours, and ultimately our destiny. A circle can be a **mirror** or a **maze**. It can reflect your highest truth or trap your deepest doubt.

The great shift happens when we no longer seek **validation**—a nod of approval to ease our inner doubt—but seek **elevation**—a mirror that challenges, expands, and awakens us.

The Story of Anna and the Mountain Fire Circle

Anna was a gifted ceramic artist living in a quiet coastal town, where salt hung in the air and routine hummed like a lullaby. Her days were filled with the warmth of her kiln and the scent of wet clay, but her **soul ached for more**—a longing not just to make objects, but to **heal lives through the ritual of creation**.

She dreamed of building a sanctuary—a sacred space where art met spirit, where hands could shape not just clay, but trauma, memory, and renewal.

Yet every time she shared this dream with the people she grew up with—friends who cared deeply but thought small—she was met with well-intentioned resistance.

"You already have a shop. Why gamble with something so uncertain?"

"Sounds beautiful, but people don't really pay for that."

"You're too sensitive for the kind of world that would support this."

And so Anna shrank.

Not because she lacked vision—

but because her circle echoed her **doubt**, not her **destiny**.

Her days continued like waves on the shore: repetitive, predictable, and slowly eroding her fire.

Until one autumn evening.

She attended a regional art retreat up in the hills. Among strangers and silence, she felt oddly free. That's where she met **Eli**, a sculptor known for his wild, asymmetrical installations—and his **startling stillness**.

Eli didn't ask about sales or strategy.

He simply looked at her latest piece—a bowl cracked intentionally down the centre—and said:

"What would your clay say… if you stopped silencing it?"

That single question shattered the dam within her.

No one had ever asked her what the **clay** felt like.

What **it** wanted to express.

What **truth** she was hiding in form.

She broke down that night—not from weakness, but from release.

In the months that followed, Anna began attending Eli's gatherings—circles of artists and seekers who didn't just share techniques; they shared **truth**.

These were not your typical workshops.

They met by firelight in a converted barn high in the mountains. There were no stages, no applause, no egos. Only raw questions, deep listening, and **sacred discomfort.**

They didn't flatter each other; they **challenged mediocrity.**

They didn't offer advice; they **held space for emergence.**

They didn't demand perfection; they **honoured the honest.**

And slowly, Anna transformed.

Not in skill—she had always been gifted.

But in **energy, clarity, and courage.**

Being surrounded by those who spoke to her **soul and not her fear,** who reminded her that sensitivity was not a liability but a superpower—

she began to believe in the voice her clay had always whispered.

Within a year, Anna opened her sanctuary.

It was nestled on the edge of a forest, overlooking the sea. There was no formal sign, just a carved piece of driftwood that read:

"Hands that heal."

People came—not for products, but for presence. They moulded clay, sat in stillness, and left something of their pain behind in the fire.

Anna didn't just build a space.

She built a **living altar of transformation**, born not from ambition but from **alignment**.

And it all began when she stepped out of the fog of familiarity and into a **circle of fire**.

Reflection

Sometimes your dream doesn't need more planning—it needs a new ecosystem.
One that doesn't fear your light.
One that doesn't mistake your intuition for instability.
One that sees your soul before your résumé.

1. How to Identify Draining vs. Elevating Circles

Draining Circles:

- Operate from fear, scarcity, or competition
- Shame ambition, or spiritual inquiry
- Celebrate only comfort or conformity
- Gossip more than grow
- Keep score instead of keeping space

Elevating Circles:

- Honour vulnerability as strength

- Ask better questions than they offer answers
- Hold you accountable to your highest potential
- Celebrate your wins even when you're struggling
- Make space for silence, depth, and growth

Litmus Test:

"Do I feel more alive, more courageous, more myself after time with them?"

Or:

"Do I shrink, second-guess, or suppress who I truly am?"

2. How to Nurture and Grow High-Value Circles

Great circles are not found. They are **forged**.

They are born in:

- Shared values
- Earned trust
- Emotional generosity
- A commitment to growth over gossip

Practical Practices:

- Host a monthly salon or gathering where the focus is on truth, not titles

- Create rituals (not routines) around storytelling, honest check-ins, or joint creation
- Ask deeper questions like:

"What is life asking of you right now?"

"What is the truth you're afraid to say out loud?"

- Offer help before it's asked.
- Celebrate others' breakthroughs with presence, not performance.

Remember, circles grow when you stop keeping score and start **holding space**.

3. How to Contribute: Become the Flame, Not the Fog

You don't attract powerful circles by chasing them. You become one of them by becoming someone who **lights fires** in others.

- Speak truth kindly but firmly
- Celebrate other people's light even when yours is dim
- Be consistent: emotional availability, not just cleverness
- Share from your heart, not your highlight reel
- Apologise when you falter, and forgive freely

In a high-value circle, your **rawness is not a liability—it's currency.**

The Fire Pit vs. The Fog Machine

Imagine two types of gatherings.

One is a fire pit.

It's warm, real, raw. People gather close, share stories, and cook dreams over the flame. They emerge smelling of smoke and truth.

The other is a fog machine.

It's dramatic, but shallow. The air is dense with pretence. Visibility is low. You can't see yourself clearly, let alone others. It chokes the real and worships the image.

Every relationship, every circle, is one or the other.

You must ask:

"Am I gathering with fire-makers or fog-bearers?"

"And more importantly—what am I bringing?"

The Spiritual Truth

True circles are not just support systems. They are **soul contracts**.

They remind you that your dream is valid. That your voice matters. That your growth is not arrogance—it's *alignment*.

When you're surrounded by people who see the **sacred in your striving**, you no longer need to explain your fire.

Reflection

"The people you surround yourself with will either tether you to yesterday or awaken the architecture of tomorrow inside you."

You do not owe everyone access to your becoming.

Curate your circle like you would your altar—with reverence.

Exercises & Journal Prompts

1. **Circle Mapping**:
    - List the five people you spend the most emotional time with.
    - Do they feed your fears or your future?

2. **Energy Audit**:
    - After spending time with someone, write down how you *feel*—more expanded or contracted?

3. **Contribution Check**:
    - Ask yourself: *"Would I want to be in a circle led by me?"*

4. **Action Step**:
    - Invite 2-3 people for a gathering where you ask deeper questions than you ever have.

The Mirrors We Walk With

In what ways do your relationships reflect your inner world, and how can intentional connections accelerate your rise?

There's a quiet truth no one tells you in your early years: **The people you surround yourself with are not just companions—they are mirrors.**

Some show you the parts of yourself you've hidden. Others reflect the self you're too afraid to become. And a rare few? They hold the mirror steady when you're ready to truly see.

Jonah and the Quiet Window

Jonah was a systems thinker. In spreadsheets, in plans, in the timing of his morning coffee, he sought comfort in precision. Life, for him, was about logic. Order. Clean answers. He had built a successful consulting practice by the age of thirty-five, but no amount of growth in his bank account could quiet the gnawing emptiness in his chest.

His relationships were functional but hollow—colleagues, contacts, acquaintances. Conversations felt like transactions. Celebrations felt like obligations. Even love felt measured, like a performance of connection rather than its raw experience.

He once said to a therapist, half-joking:

"I'm the architect of a beautiful house no one wants to live in—not even me."

That statement lingered.

One fall, during a business retreat in Kyoto, Jonah stayed at a monastery turned guesthouse. The rooms were sparse. The meals, simple. The silence, immense.

Each morning, an elderly monk named Kaoru would clean the windows of the meditation hall. Jonah noticed him from the garden bench. Every day. Same cloth. Same deliberate movements.

Curious, Jonah asked, "Why clean a window that's already clear?"

Kaoru smiled and replied:

"The glass may be clean to the eye. But the **dust of yesterday's weather still dims the morning sun.** We clean not just for clarity—but to stay present with what is now."

That answer cracked something open.

Over tea, Kaoru explained a principle that became a cornerstone of Jonah's transformation:

"We think our relationships are with other people. But they are always first with ourselves.

Who you allow close is a reflection of what you believe you're worthy of.

Who you chase is often a reflection of what part of you still feels unloved.

And whom you avoid? Often the part of you you're not yet ready to face."

Jonah went quiet. His mind raced with the names of people he had let into his life—not out of resonance, but convenience. Not out of alignment, but the image.

He realised he had mastered efficiency, but avoided intimacy. He knew how to solve problems, but not how to **be seen**.

The Inner Rebuild

Over the next year, Jonah did something radical.

He stopped reaching out to people who made him shrink, no matter how useful they once were.

He stopped "networking" in the traditional sense, and started seeking **mirrors**—people who challenged his soul, not just complimented his skills.

He joined a circle of entrepreneurs who didn't just talk metrics, but meaning. Who asked:

- "What does your success cost your peace?"
- "Where are you compromising your soul for scale?"
- "What story are you still living that no longer fits your truth?"

For the first time, Jonah cried in front of strangers.

And they stayed.

Not to fix him. But to witness him.

And from that witnessing, came an unfurling of deeper confidence, creativity, and clarity.

The Garden Gate

Imagine your life as a **walled garden**.

Each relationship is like a vine that climbs its edge.

Some vines strengthen the walls, adding beauty and protection.
Others weaken them, digging into the stone, cracking your foundation.

And yet, most of us leave the garden gate wide open—unconsciously letting anyone in.

But once you become aware of your inner world—your values, your wounds, your vision—you begin to **curate** that garden. You pull the weeds. You invite in pollinators. You build benches for those who make the space more alive.

And in time, your inner harmony becomes mirrored in your outer world.

Insight

The rise you're seeking—in career, in purpose, in wealth—is never a solo ascent.

It is accelerated or delayed by the **relational architecture** you build around you.

Surround yourself with those who:

- Call you forward, not just comfort your past.
- See your blind spots, not just your brilliance.
- Love your truth, even when it's inconvenient.

Because the people you walk with are not a background to your story—they are **the frequency you rise to.**

Reflection Questions & Exercises

1. **Relationship Audit**
    - Who are the five people you speak to most often?
    - What do you feel *after* you speak to them—drained or expanded?

2. **The Mirror Letter**
    - Write a letter from your higher self. What kind of people would *they* keep close?
    - What would they no longer tolerate, excuse, or chase?

3. **Intentional Circles**
    - Seek out or create a community that holds your soul accountable.
    - Look for spaces that value **depth over display**, **truth over tactics**, and **evolution over ego**.

4. **Energetic Boundaries**
    - Practice saying "no" without explanation for one draining commitment this week.
    - Use the energy saved to deepen one authentic connection.

CHAPTER VI

From Breakdown to Breakthrough

"Sometimes life has to fall apart so you can rise with what truly matters."

— Shree Shambav

Synopsis

From Breakdown to Breakthrough reveals the hidden wisdom that lives inside failure. While society glorifies success, it often overlooks the pain, loss, and collapse that precede meaningful transformation. This section guides readers to see breakdowns not as endings but as sacred openings. By embracing discomfort and reframing low points as initiations, we uncover the courage, humility, and clarity needed to rise. Here, rock bottom becomes solid ground, pain becomes fuel, and every fall becomes a setup for a more aligned ascent. It's not the breakdown that defines us—but what we do with it.

The Alchemy of the Fall

How personal failures serve as catalysts for deeper transformation and long-term success

"A broken bone grows back stronger. So does a broken spirit—if it's allowed to heal with truth."

Lena and the Unfinished Bridge

Lena was an ambitious architect in her early thirties, known for designing sleek, efficient structures for urban skylines. She had always been a high-achiever—valedictorian, scholarship student, and rapid promotions in her firm. Her mind worked like scaffolding: neat, logical, with plans laid out in blueprints.

Her dream project was a suspension bridge across a river in her hometown—a symbolic and personal design intended to connect two long-separated communities. It was her gift back to the place that raised her. The project received attention, funding, and even international recognition *before* a single beam was laid.

But then it collapsed. Not the bridge—the **project**.

A flaw in the initial structural analysis, missed during peer review, led to delays, public embarrassment, lawsuits, and the loss of her professional license.

The fall from grace was swift. Headlines read:

"Golden Girl's Bridge to Nowhere."

Her reputation crumbled. Her confidence was shattered. Her savings evaporated. But worse than the public failure was the **inner silence** that followed.

For the first time in her life, Lena had no plan.

Failure as Initiation, Not Punishment

In many ways, **Lena's failure was not a punishment—it was a portal.**

She moved back home, ashamed and hollow. Her father, a retired woodworker, said something to her one night under the porch light:

"You built so much for the world. Now build something for yourself. And let it take time. Slow wood doesn't crack."

That phrase lingered.

Lena stopped trying to "fix" the past and began to *listen* to it.

She realised she had always been building to be seen—by critics, boards, and awards—but never truly *felt* by herself. She had become an architect of perfection but not of presence.

The Inner Blueprint

In solitude, Lena studied again—not engineering this time, but philosophy, meditation, poetry, and the psychology of shame. She volunteered to design a community garden, then a schoolyard playground. Not to redeem her reputation, but to reconnect with meaning.

She met failure not as an enemy, but as a **mentor who stripped away all that was inessential.**

The turning point came three years later—not when she returned to architecture—but when she began **teaching**

design to formerly incarcerated youth, helping them draw not just buildings, but visions for their lives.

She used her failure as a **bridge**, just not the one she thought she'd build.

The Crucible and the Gold

Think of your life like raw ore mined from deep within the earth.

Failure is the **crucible**—the intense heat that separates gold from grit.

When we avoid or suppress failure, we carry the weight of unrefined experience.

But when we *enter* the fire consciously—questioning, grieving, learning—something rare emerges.

Not just knowledge.

Wisdom.

Not just recovery.

Redirection.

Like alchemists of old, we don't escape the darkness—we **transmute** it.

What Failure Gives You (If You Let It)

- **Humility without self-hatred** – the ability to kneel before truth without collapsing under it.

- **Clarity without cynicism** – seeing the cracks in your past thinking, but not defining yourself by them.

- **Empathy born from experience** – because once you've been broken, you become gentler with others' wounds.

- **Resilience rooted in surrender** – not the fight to bounce back, but the faith to rebuild with depth.

From Breakdown to Breakthrough

Many of the world's most revered souls—creators, leaders, visionaries—trace their transformation not to triumphs, but to the moment everything **fell apart**:

- Nelson Mandela's prison years did not crush him— they refined his clarity.

- Oprah's early failures as a news anchor led her to a deeper platform of authenticity.

Why? Because **failure unravels the ego**, and in that unravelling, the soul can finally speak.

Reflection Questions

1. What failure have you been defining yourself by?
    - What if it wasn't a definition, but an *initiation*?

2. What truth did failure reveal to you that success never could?

3. In what ways did the breakdown point you toward what is most essential in your life?

4. If your failure was your teacher, what would its lesson plan look like?

Exercises

1. The Forgiveness Letter

Write a letter from your future self, thanking your past self for that failure. List what it helped you see, change, or grow through.

2. The Fire Journal

Take one experience of deep personal failure and journal through these prompts:

- What was lost?
- What was revealed?
- What was rebuilt?
- What part of you emerged stronger?

3. The Alchemy Map

Draw a three-part map:

- **Stage 1:** The Fall (What happened?)

- **Stage 2:** The Fire (What emotions did you face?)
- **Stage 3:** The Forge (What strength, wisdom, or clarity emerged?)

Label it: *"The Bridge I Didn't Know I Was Building."*

Thought

"Failure does not end your story.

It edits your manuscript so the truest chapter can begin."

If we allow it, **our greatest collapse can be our most sacred reconstruction.**

We are not defined by what broke us, but by how we *chose to rebuild*—with softness, with wisdom, and with the quiet confidence of those who have met the fire and learned to sing in its heat.

The Furnace and the Flame

Reframing pain into purpose: how emotional resilience becomes power

"Pain is not the enemy. It is the midwife of transformation. And those who learn to sit with it—not flee from it—emerge with fire in their bones, and a tenderness that cannot be faked."

Kai and the Hollow Tree

Kai grew up in a mountain village, cradled by cedar trees and silence. His mother used to say, *"Everything broken in the world was once trying to grow."* As a child, Kai didn't understand what she meant.

But life, as it always does, explained it later—with **pain**.

At seventeen, Kai lost both his parents in a landslide that buried half the village. Grief hollowed him out like the trees that stood stripped bare after the storm—sturdy on the outside, empty within. He stopped speaking for almost a year. People called it shock. But deep inside, it was **grief that had no language yet**.

He spent his twenties drifting. Not aimless—but aching. Trying to fill the silence with work, movement, service, noise.

Then one day, while helping rebuild a nearby school after a fire, he noticed a boy sitting alone. Crying, but not loudly. Just curled up, breathing slowly, like grief had become a rhythm in his body.

Kai didn't say anything. He just sat beside him. After a while, the boy leaned against his shoulder. They stayed like that for a long time.

That moment changed Kai's life.

Not because something grand happened—but because he realised something **profound**:

His pain had given him a language that only the suffering could understand.

Pain as Compost, Not Curse

Most people treat pain as a **contaminant**—something to eliminate, deny, numb, or spiritually bypass.

But true transformation begins when we see pain not as poison, but as **compost**—dense, dark, rich material that can feed something sacred.

It is not the pain itself that grows us. It is what we **do with it.**

- Some let pain harden them into cynicism.
- Others let it hollow them into wisdom.

The difference lies in **resilience**—not the toughness to resist pain, but the *tenderness to stay with it long enough to understand it.*

The Broken Pot and the Golden Vein

In Japanese culture, there is an art form called **Kintsugi**—the mending of broken pottery with gold.

The cracks are not hidden; they are **highlighted**.

The wound becomes the most valuable part of the object. It says: *"This was broken, yes. But it broke open—not apart."*

In the same way, our suffering—when met with presence and healing—becomes our *signature strength.*

The places where we cracked become the veins through which wisdom flows.

Resilience: The Soul's Quiet Power

True power doesn't roar. It whispers.

- It's the **single mother** who keeps showing up with softness.
- The **survivor** who uses their pain to comfort others in silence.
- The **artist** who turns heartbreak into beauty.
- The **teacher** who listens harder because they were never heard.

Resilience is not about avoiding breakdowns. It is about *returning*—again and again—with grace, even if your hands still shake.

And in this returning, power is born—not the power to control, but the power to **heal, create, and lift others**.

Reframing Pain into Purpose: The Process

1. **Witness** – Sit with the pain. Do not judge or interpret too quickly. Let it speak.
2. **Name** – What was the truth you ignored that pain finally revealed?
3. **Extract** – What strength emerged *only* because of that suffering?

4. **Redirect** – Who else might benefit from the path you've walked?

5. **Build** – Use it. Channel it into a creation, a service, a story, a system.

Pain must move. If not, it festers.

But when you give it **motion**, it becomes **meaning**.

Kai's Return

Years later, Kai opened a retreat centre named *The Hollow Tree*.

Not a place of luxury, but of **listening**—for people who had lost something they couldn't name.

There were no gurus. No promises. Just fire circles, silence, shared meals, and deep honesty.

His pain had not left him.

But it no longer controlled him.

It had become his **flame**—quiet, steady, warming others in the coldest seasons of their lives.

Reflection Questions

1. What pain in your life have you tried to bury, but still lingers in the background?

2. What skill, sensitivity, or strength has emerged *because* of that pain?

3. Who could benefit if you shared that experience with courage and compassion?

4. What would it look like to **honour your wounds**, not hide them?

Soul Exercises

1. Wound to Wisdom Timeline

Draw a timeline of your life. Mark the painful chapters.

Next to each, write one **strength** or **insight** that emerged from that season.

2. The Golden Letter

Write a letter to the version of yourself that was in the middle of that pain. Tell them what they couldn't see yet. Thank them for surviving.

3. The Service Seed

Identify one way you can use your story or pain to serve others.

Is it a support group, an article, a song, a mentorship, a poem, a retreat?

The Tree and the Storm

A tree that survives a storm grows deeper roots.

Its branches may break. Its leaves may fall. But underground, something stronger anchors it to the earth.

You are not fragile. You are rooted.

The winds may bend you. The rain may blind you.

But when the storm passes, what remains is the *truth*.

And truth—earned through pain—is the strongest wood we build a legacy from.

The Echo in the Well

Internal dialogues and belief shifts are required to convert rock bottom into a turning point.

"Rock bottom isn't the end. It's the echo chamber where you finally hear your soul speak without interruption."

Rhea and the Silent Well

Rhea was once the voice behind other people's dreams. A ghostwriter for celebrities, a quiet strategist for brands, a behind-the-scenes alchemist of other people's success.

On the outside, she had it all—prestige, steady income, applause from the shadows.

But inside, she felt like an echo without a voice of her own.

It all collapsed the day her long-term partner left and her biggest client dropped her.

In a week, she lost her relationship, her livelihood, and the carefully constructed identity she thought was hers.

Rhea fell—hard.

She moved back to her childhood town, into a dusty attic above her uncle's garage.

She stopped writing. Stopped speaking.

Her phone gathered dust like a relic from another life.

Each night she'd lie awake staring at the wooden beams, asking questions in silence:

- *"Was any of it real?"*
- *"What if I was only ever valuable because I made others shine?"*
- *"Who am I without the role?"*

And one night, from the silence came a whisper—not from outside, but within:

"If you've hit the bottom, then stop digging. Start listening."

That whisper became a turning point.

The Inner Earthquake: Rock Bottom Isn't Failure, It's Fracture

Rock bottom is not the death of possibility. It's the **rupture of illusion.**

It's when the scaffolding built by ego and expectations collapses, and for the first time…

You meet yourself—raw, trembling, unmasked.

Most of us fear that moment because it feels like annihilation. But in truth, it is initiation.

Not into despair—but into **authentic selfhood**.

Just like a seed must crack open underground before it can reach the light, the soul often awakens through collapse, not comfort.

The Crater and the Compass

When a meteor hits the Earth, it leaves a crater.

Destructive. Violent. Shocking.

But over time, those craters become lakes.

Lush ecosystems. Birthplaces of beauty.

Rock bottom is your **internal crater**, left by impact, but brimming with the chance to fill with clarity.

And within that crater, if you listen closely, is buried your **true compass**.

The voice that doesn't ask, *"How do I survive?"*

But instead asks, *"What must I now become?"*

The Three Inner Dialogues That Must Shift

1. From "I've lost everything" → "I've been stripped to my truth."

Loss feels like annihilation until you realise what's been lost was not essential—just *familiar*.

- The job was your identity, not your purpose.
- The relationship was your safety net, not your source.
- The version of you that shattered was a costume—not your soul.

New Belief: *"This is not death. It's disrobing."*

2. From "Why me?" → "What now?"

"Why me?" locks you in victimhood.

"What now?" opens the door to possibility.

You don't need answers to heal.

You need **agency**. A small next step. A reclaimed choice.

New Belief: *"I am not powerless. I am present. And presence births power."*

3. From "I am broken" → "I am breaking open."

Pain cracks your container not to destroy you—but to expand your capacity.

To love deeper.

To see clearly.

To rise truer.

New Belief: *"This pain is not punishment. It is the portal."*

Rhea's Voice

Rhea began journaling not for clients—but for herself.

Messy pages. Honest prayers. Letters to her past and her future.

She didn't try to monetise her healing.

She honoured it.

Eventually, those journal entries became essays.

Then talks.

Then a memoir that touched thousands—not because it was polished, but because it was **real**.

Her rock bottom didn't kill her voice.

It carved it.

And that voice, once buried in the noise of others, now echoed in others' healing.

Practical Exercises: Transmuting Despair into Direction

1. The Bottom Letter

Write a letter *from* your rock bottom self to your future self. Let the rawness speak.

Then, write a response *from* your future healed self. Watch the dialogue reveal hidden wisdom.

2. Identify the False Identity

List what was lost during your fall.

Beside each, ask: *Was this truly me, or something I used to be seen/validated?*

This reveals the illusion's pain burned away.

3. Create a 'What Now' Map

Draw a circle in the centre: "Me, Now."

Branch out into micro-actions: Who can I reach out to? What 1 thing can I reclaim?

It's not about fixing everything. Just anchoring back into movement.

The Diamond and the Depth

Diamonds aren't found on mountaintops.

They are discovered deep within the **earth's pressure** zones.

Their beauty is born from compression.

Their clarity from time in the dark.

So too, your truest power—your unshakable voice—emerges not in the light, but in the long night.

Rock bottom is not the end. It is the place where pressure births diamonds, where silence births clarity, and where the broken ground becomes sacred soil.

The Grace in the Fall

How surrender, rather than resistance, enables growth during collapse.

Daniel and the Ash Tree

Daniel was a master craftsman—his hands shaped wood the way rivers shape stones: slowly, lovingly, leaving stories in the grain. His small workshop, nestled between the hills and the woods, was his sanctuary. He had built a reputation for creating furniture not just with skill, but with soul.

One day, a wildfire ravaged the hillside. The trees he'd grown up walking beneath—his muses—were reduced to smouldering silhouettes. His workshop, his tools, even his late father's carving bench—ashes.

He stood before the ruins, fists clenched, heart screaming in silence.

All that effort, all those years—gone in a night of fire.

For weeks, Daniel fought the grief. He tried to rebuild from memory, but every board he cut felt like betrayal. Every attempt to recreate the past only deepened the void.

Then one morning, wandering among the blackened woods, he sat beneath a charred ash tree.

There was nothing to do. Nowhere to go. So he just... sat. He exhaled for the first time in weeks. He stopped fighting.

And in that stillness, something subtle happened.

He noticed a tiny green shoot, curling up from the base of the burned tree.

Life—tender, defiant—was returning.

And within Daniel, too, something shifted.

It wasn't that the pain left—it was that **he stopped resisting the pain**.

He surrendered—not in defeat, but in trust.

Not in passivity, but in profound receptivity.

Surrender: Not Weakness, But Wisdom

Surrender is not giving up.

It's giving in—to something deeper.

It's the moment the swimmer, caught in a riptide, realises that fighting the current only leads to drowning. Instead, they **float**, allowing the water to carry them until they can reorient.

Surrender is the art of **yielding without abandoning**.

It's trusting that beneath the collapse, there is a current that still flows.

"Sometimes, the greatest strength is the courage to fall—to fall inward, to fall open."

The Bow and the Release

Think of a bow and arrow.

To launch forward, the string must be pulled back.

The more tension, the farther the reach.

But the release—the **letting go**—is what allows the arrow to fly.

In life, we often resist the pullback. We cling to what was.

We tighten our grip in fear.

But transformation doesn't come from *holding on* to the bowstring.

It comes from trusting the aim and *releasing*.

Resistance vs. Surrender: The Inner Dialogue

Resistance Says	Surrender Whispers
"This shouldn't be happening."	"What is this trying to teach me?"
"I must fix this immediately."	"I will listen before I act."
"I'm failing."	"I am unfolding."
"I can't handle this."	"This too belongs. Let it pass through."

Surrender doesn't bypass reality. It deepens our presence within it.

It doesn't deny the storm. It lets us find the **eye** of the storm.

Daniel's Renewal

Daniel returned to his workshop—not with plans to rebuild what was, but to *respond to what is*.

He began crafting from the charred remains.

Burnt beams became altar tables.

Ashen wood became sculptures that whispered resilience.

His art now held a fire-etched story.

People came not just for his skill—but for the stillness his work carried.

He hadn't risen *in spite of* the collapse. He had risen *through* it.

Practical Reflections and Exercises

1. The Storm Journal

Draw a storm cloud on a page. Write within it all you're resisting right now.

Beneath the cloud, draw a river. Ask: *What if I flowed with this instead of against it?*

Write three truths you might learn if you allowed the discomfort to speak.

2. The Bow Exercise

Close your eyes and visualise yourself as a bow being drawn back.

Feel the tension, the resistance.

Now, release.

Feel yourself moving forward, not from effort—but from alignment and trust.

3. Surrender Statements

Repeat these aloud when caught in resistance:

- *"I allow this moment to be what it is."*
- *"I trust the timing of my unfolding."*
- *"Even this is part of my becoming."*

The Lotus Beneath the Mud

The lotus doesn't bloom in clear water.

It rises from the depths of still, murky, messy mud.

Not by fighting the darkness—but by **trusting the reach** of its inner light.

Surrender is the sunlight the soul leans toward when everything else has been stripped away.

It's the quiet knowing that even in ruin, something sacred is trying to bloom.

Arup and the Temple of the Unseen Flame

A story of sacred refinement, not failure

Years after rising from the ashes of his earlier collapse in commerce and creative chaos, Arup stood once more at a threshold. Not the dramatic brink of crisis—but a quieter, more mysterious edge. One that doesn't arrive with noise, but with an unnerving stillness.

The sanctuary he had built—had become a refuge for seekers, creatives, and leaders yearning for depth beyond performance. It was born from fire and faith, from his hard-won truths. But now… something had shifted.

There was no scandal. No catastrophe.

Just a subtle thinning.

Programs once vibrant now echoed with polite detachment. The community that once pulsed with life grew ghostly. Support wavered. Energy waned. The space still stood—but the **soul had stepped out**.

Arup had done everything by the sacred playbook.

Vision. Value. Visibility.

He had honoured both the strategy and the silence.

And yet—the light was dimming.

At first, he resisted.

He redesigned. Reinvited. Reignited.

But something in him knew:

He was trying to breathe life into a form whose purpose had been fulfilled.

One misty morning, while walking barefoot along the damp forest trail behind Aprameya Hall, he noticed the old Peepal tree. The one whose branches had once canopied their morning chants. It had fallen—its roots exposed, trunk hollowed. The same tree that adorned their logo. Now quiet, broken, strangely beautiful in surrender.

Arup didn't grieve. He simply knelt beside it.

Not to fix. Not to interpret. Just to be with it.

And in that stillness, the tree whispered something only his heart could hear:

"You are not here to preserve temples.

You are here to tend the living flame."

In that moment, he understood.

The retreat was never the destination.

It was one chapter in a sacred unfolding.

So, he let go—not in resignation, but in **reverence**.

He didn't collapse. He released.

He stopped chasing metrics.

He started writing again—pen to page, soul to sky.

He met with fewer people, but spoke with rawness and realness.

He returned not to stages, but to stone circles by firelight, where truth still trembled.

And then—without effort or push—something arrived.

A letter.

A publisher.

An invitation.

But not for a book on leadership tactics or scaling wisdom. They asked for the real work. The unseen work.

The legacy hidden beneath legacy.

A book on **invisible capital**. On **frequency**. On **sacred surrender**.

Arup smiled.

Not because he was finally seen.

But because he had finally **become so still**,

that truth found him again.

An Invitation - the Reader

Your stillness is not stagnation.

It may be a sacred pause to realign your compass.

Your softening is not weakness.

It may be the strength to honour seasons that are shifting.

And your letting go is not the end.

It is the threshold of your next becoming.

Like Arup, you are not here to carry monuments.

You are here to carry the flame.

So tend it gently.

Let the fallen tree show you when to stop striving.

Let the silence remind you who you are beneath your efforts.

Let the surrender bless you with the next message meant just for you.

"There are some truths too soft to shout—

they wait for the one who finally stops running."

May your fire burn, not to impress,

but to **illumine**.

May your legacy rise, not from what you clung to—

but from what you were brave enough to release.

CHAPTER VII

Rituals of the Wealthy and Wise

"Silence isn't the absence of action—it's the origin of all wise action."

— Shree Shambav

Synopsis

Rituals of the Wealthy and Wise explores the hidden architecture behind consistent excellence. True power and prosperity are rarely the result of luck—they're cultivated through invisible habits, thoughtful routines, and deep inner alignment. This section reveals how the most successful individuals structure their mornings, protect their solitude, and build inner sanctuaries for reflection and clarity. It also unveils the often-overlooked value of sacred stillness and disciplined decision-making. These rituals aren't restrictive; they're liberating. They transform time into focus, rest into strategy, and learning into legacy. The difference between chaos and calm, noise and wisdom, is often found in the rituals we repeat.

The Dawn Architects — How You Begin Shapes Who You Become

"Every morning is a vote for the life you say you want."

— From *The Silent Forces That Shape Destiny*

The Silent Sculptor of Destiny

Imagine your life as a grand sculpture.

Each day is a fresh chisel mark—delicate, intentional, powerful. And every morning, before the noise, before the requests, before the world intrudes—there is a rare stillness. That is when the sculptor arrives.

The question is: **Will you meet them? Or sleep through their visit?**

Because morning is not just the start of your day—it is the **spiritual architect** of your life.

The world speaks of hustle. Of racing into the day with caffeine and chaos. But beneath the noise, mystics, monks, masters, and makers of every age have known this:

Your first hour is not just a habit.

It is a **signal to the universe** about how you treat your inner temple.

The Story of Arup and the Flamekeeper's Hour

After his quiet return from the spotlight, Arup no longer began his mornings with emails or analytics. Instead, he rose before the sun, barefoot on the cool stone of his quiet home near the forest edge.

He called it the **Flamekeeper's Hour**.

It wasn't glamorous.

It wasn't optimised.

It was sacred.

A brass lamp.

A page of handwritten reflections.

A slow breath that met the dawn with reverence.

Sometimes silence. Sometimes a chant. Sometimes just watching the light change on the wall.

And in those small acts, he found a strange clarity—not the kind that screams certainty, but the kind that whispers direction.

As weeks turned to seasons, he realised something:

He was no longer reacting to life. He was conversing with it.

His days, though filled with tasks, felt less burdened.

Decisions came clearer.

People felt his groundedness.

He was building—not from exhaustion, but from **alignment**.

Why Morning Rituals Matter (Even When No One Sees Them)

Think of an **arrow**.

Before it soars, it is pulled **back**—in stillness, in silence. The energy built in the backward motion is what gives it direction and speed.

Mornings are that sacred draw.

Not every day is perfect. Not every breath will feel enlightened. But over time, these subtle choices accumulate into a **frequency**—a vibration of discipline, intention, and depth that shapes your entire being.

You don't rise successful.

You rise sacred.

And that sacredness—practised daily—becomes your **inner compass** when life throws storms.

Analogies of the Morning Mindset

- **A seed watered every morning** eventually becomes a forest. But miss a few days in the early stages, and the sprout may die without anyone noticing.
- **A tuning fork** struck each dawn keeps the entire instrument of your life in harmony.
- **A prayer whispered at dawn** echoes louder than a thousand to-do lists shouted at noon.

Sacred vs Superficial Discipline

Discipline is not about punishing yourself into productivity.

Real discipline is *devotion*.

It's how you romance your own soul.

How you tell your life: "You matter enough for me to show up early, gently, quietly."

True morning rituals aren't loud. They're not about checking boxes. They're about **checking in—with your breath, your body, your being.**

What Happens When You Skip It?

When you skip your morning ritual, nothing catastrophic happens that day.

But **slowly**, you become a stranger to yourself.

You check your phone before you check your pulse.

You scroll before you sit.

You consume before you create.

And without realising it, your life becomes a reaction—rather than a response.

Designing Your Morning: The Inner Fire Blueprint

Not all rituals are for everyone. But all of us need **a gatekeeper between sleep and speed.**

Here's a framework inspired by Arup's sacred hour:

The Four Flames of Morning Practice

1. **Flame of Stillness** – Silence, meditation, prayer.
2. **Flame of Expression** – Journaling, art, longhand writing.

3. **Flame of Movement** – Gentle yoga, stretching, breathwork.

4. **Flame of Direction** – Reading something sacred, reviewing goals, or setting a clear intention.

You don't need all four daily. But one flame, well-tended, can ignite your whole life.

A Reflection

Success is not a race to a distant summit.

It is a daily reunion—with who you truly are.

Morning rituals remind you that before the world tells you what to do, **you get to decide who you are becoming**.

And if you honour the mornings, the day will begin to honour you.

Exercise: Tending to Your Sacred Hour

1. **Name Your Morning**: Give your morning ritual a personal title. Not "routine," but something poetic—like "The Hour of Becoming" or "Return to Source." Naming makes it sacred.

2. **Design Your 20-Minute Flow**: Choose one still practice, one expressive act, and one breath-based movement to begin. Even 20 minutes is powerful when done with presence.

3. **Track the Feeling, Not the Habit**: Instead of checking boxes, reflect each evening: *Did I feel more grounded? Less reactive?* Let feeling be your feedback.

"Mornings are where destiny rehearses quietly—before the world takes the stage."

The Compass Beneath the Storm — The Forgotten Power of Stillness

"In a world addicted to speed, silence is a rebellious clarity."

— from *The Silent Forces That Shape Destiny*

The Storm and the Compass

Imagine you're on a sailboat mid-ocean, the sky grey and the waves loud with unrest. Wind howls. Your sails flap. The radio blares conflicting coordinates.

Everyone's shouting directions.

Now picture yourself clutching the compass—but it's spinning erratically.

This is what modern life often feels like: **decisions made in storms, with broken instruments, amidst noise mistaken for urgency.**

But if you cut the engine…

If you drop anchor…

If you sit with the sea…

The compass stills.

That stillness—**not movement**—is when direction becomes clear.

Arup and the Three-Day Silence

After the launch of his third creative platform—a digital ecosystem combining education, art, and healing—Arup found himself strangely restless.

Everything seemed to be working externally:

User engagement was up.

The press was calling.

Collaborators were applauding.

But *inside*, something felt misaligned. It wasn't burnout. It wasn't fear. It was **noise**—subtle, incessant, and dulling.

So, without announcement or planning, Arup disappeared into a small hut near the edge of the forest where an old Zen monk once lived. Just a backpack, a notebook, and three days of intentional solitude.

No devices. No books. No voices but wind and birds.

The first day, his mind rebelled—racing with incomplete tasks and unspoken fears.

The second day, it wept—long-held grief rising without narrative.

The third day, silence arrived—not the absence of sound, but the presence of **truth**.

That morning, sitting cross-legged in soft light, a phrase surfaced in his inner ear:

"The signal lives beneath the static."

He knew what he had to let go of.

He knew what he had to build next.

Not because someone advised him. But because his **soul finally had room to speak**.

Why Stillness Clarifies, and Noise Corrupts

Noise confuses.

Speed blinds.

Endless input drowns the voice that matters most—your *inner voice*.

Stillness isn't laziness. It's the **sacred pause before precision**.

Like a bow drawn before release.

Like a seed resting in soil before emergence.

Like a heart stilled before speaking the truth.

In stillness, you don't react—you *respond*.

You listen—not just to your logic, but to your **intuition, your body, your knowing**.

And that's where wisdom waits. Not in the whirlwind of opinions, but in the **echo of your own breath**.

Solitude: The Mirror Room of the Soul

Solitude is not loneliness. It is a *sacred company* with its own essence.

Think of the **great visionaries**—Jesus in the desert, Buddha beneath the Bodhi tree, Rumi wandering the plains, even Steve Jobs taking long solitary walks.

They didn't stumble on insight through productivity. They **courted clarity** through aloneness.

Solitude strips away performance. It removes the masks. In its nakedness, it offers you the most honest advisor you'll ever meet—your **unaltered self**.

A World Addicted to Noise

Today's world glorifies:

- 24/7 connectivity
- Instant responses
- Constant updates
- Urgency over accuracy

But clarity **does not compete with chaos**. It quietly waits beneath it.

The most life-altering decisions—whether to leave, begin, pause, or say yes—**do not arise in crowded rooms or during dopamine scrolls**.

They come when you've slowed down enough to hear the subtle whisper of inner alignment.

Arup's Compass Principle

After his forest retreat, Arup established what he later taught as the **Compass Principle** to his students:

"Never make a big decision in motion. Make it in stillness. Confirm it in solitude. Act only when your body and breath agree."

This was not spiritual poetry. It was strategic genius.

It saved him from wrong partnerships.

It helped him exit one venture just in time.

It led him to create his most spiritually integrated, emotionally resonant work.

The Clouded Lake

Imagine a lake after a storm. Mud stirred, leaves scattered, nothing visible.

Now imagine that same lake hours later—still, clear, reflective. You can see straight to the bottom.

Your mind is that lake.

If you keep stirring it with content, opinions, and productivity—even if they're positive—you **never see clearly.**

Stillness is how the mud settles.

Solitude is how the water clears.

And only then can you know—*not guess*—what lies beneath.

Practices for Stillness and Solitude

1. **Sacred No-Tech Mornings** – Start your day without input. Don't check your phone for at least 60 minutes.

2. **Weekly Solitude Walks** – No agenda. No playlist. Just walk and listen.

3. **Decision Delays** – For big choices, wait until you've sat with the question in silence at least twice.

4. **Silent Evenings** – One night a week, no screens, no talking. Let the evening reveal what the day concealed.

5. **Breath Anchoring** – In chaos, return to 10 conscious breaths. Your breath knows what your mind forgets.

The Invitation

What if your next level is not louder, faster, or more visible?

What if it's *quieter, truer, and slower?*

And what if the clarity you're seeking is already inside you—just buried beneath the noise you haven't paused to silence?

Reflection

"Stillness is not the absence of movement. It is the **presence of alignment**."

When the world rushes you, slow down.

When everyone shouts, listen deeper.

When life demands a decision—retreat first.

The wise do not rush into action.

They rest into clarity.

The Wealth of Being — How the Fulfilled Master the Art of Reflection, Rest, and Rhythm

"The truly rich are not those who possess the most—but those who pace their life to hear what most can't."

— from *The Silent Forces That Shape Destiny*

The Myth of Constant Motion

In today's world, the metric of worth is too often confused with *motion*. More meetings. More launches. More goals. More visibility.

But watch closely.

The world's most **fulfilled**, not just successful, people—those whose eyes carry peace instead of pressure—live by a deeper currency:

- **Reflection** over reaction
- **Rest** over relentless grind
- **Rhythm** over rigid hustle

They've learned something most don't:

Doing does not equal becoming.

And being is not the absence of progress—but the root of its sustainability.

The Watchmaker's Apprentice

In a quiet mountain town lived an old watchmaker named George. Known across the region for repairing ancient timepieces, he was precise, patient, and rare.

One day, a young apprentice named Rafi arrived, eager to learn.

For weeks, Rafi watched as George barely worked on the clocks. He'd take long walks. Sit in silence for hours. Sometimes, he'd hold a broken watch and just *breathe* with it.

Frustrated, Rafi asked, "Why don't you fix them? Why wait?"

George replied, "I don't fix watches. I *listen* to them until they tell me where the tension lives."

That day, Rafi learned something deeper: **the best craftsmen, healers, and visionaries don't rush into repair—they lean into rhythm.**

This is what the fulfilled know:

Reflection is not time lost—it's time wisely invested.

Why the Wealthy and Wise Honour Rhythm

Look at the deeply fulfilled:

- **The spiritual master** who wakes before dawn, not to produce, but to *be still*.
- **The conscious CEO** who blocks hours weekly not for meetings, but for *mental spaciousness*.
- **The artist or mystic** who spends more time in *silence than on stage*.

They are no less ambitious. They are more *attuned*.

They've come to understand:

Success without soul leads to collapse.

Wealth without *wavelength* leads to burnout.

And productivity without *pause* leads to a purposeless pace.

Reflection: The Inner Mirror

Reflection is how they truly fulfil and calibrate their lives. It's the mirror they hold up before making big moves.

They ask:

- *Is this aligned, or just impressive?*
- *Does this fulfil me, or only feed my image?*
- *Am I climbing the right ladder, or just the fastest one?*

Reflection prevents misalignment.

It is the **prelude to wise action.**

Rest: The Silent Multiplier

Rest isn't sleep.

It's *renewal.*

The deeply fulfilled know that **true output depends on deep input.** Their rest is sacred. It's not a reward after burnout— it's the **fuel that prevents it.**

They protect:

- Digital Sabbaths
- Naps without guilt
- Retreats that recalibrate

Because they understand:

You don't earn rest. You *need* it to stay worthy of your own mission.

They treat stillness as a source, not a side-note.

Rhythm: The Secret of the Seasons

Fulfilled individuals do not try to bloom in all seasons.

They live **cyclically**, not linearly.

Just like:

- Farmers rest their soil
- Musicians honour rests between notes
- Athletes train *and* recover

They follow **inner seasons**:

- Spring: Visioning and Initiation
- Summer: Creation and Launch
- Autumn: Harvest and Reflection
- Winter: Rest and Reinvention

They allow themselves to pause, pivot, or wait—not because they're weak, but because they're wise.

Rhythm is knowing when to rise and when to root. It is how life stays *in tune* with itself.

Arup's Return to Rhythm

After Arup's journey through collapse and surrender, what shifted was not just his strategy—but his *tempo*.

He no longer operated in a rush.

His day began with silence, not screens.

His week included "empty days," not filled calendars.

His success was measured not in metrics—but in how aligned he felt with his mission.

He had become, in essence, **a keeper of inner rhythm**.

From that space, his next work emerged—not faster, but *truer*.

Not louder, but *deeper*.

Why This Matters Now

In an age that worships acceleration, your power lies in **conscious deceleration**.

The world doesn't need more exhausted achievers.

It needs more *integrated ones*—whose pace comes from presence.

Reflection gives you direction.

Rest gives you longevity.

Rhythm gives you harmony.

Together, they birth a kind of wealth no market crash can touch.

Reflection

- Are you filling your days—or fulfilling them?
- Are you moving toward meaning—or just moving?
- Is your rhythm yours—or borrowed from someone else's urgency?

To be fulfilled is to **live in tune**.

To walk your own beat.

To know when to speak, when to act, and when to simply *listen*.

Let this be your invitation:

Not to slow down for its own sake,

But to pace yourself with **precision and peace**,

So your destiny arrives not rushed—but ready.

The River That Refused to Dry — On Lifelong Learning as Shield and Sail

"The mind that stops learning is like a well that no longer listens to rain."

— from *The Silent Forces That Shape Destiny*

The Illusion of Arrival

We are raised to believe in endpoints.

Graduate. Get the job. Master the skill. Retire. Rest.

But life is not a static trophy. It is a *moving terrain*.

And in this world—where markets shift, technology evolves, and identities blur—the ones who flourish aren't the smartest or the strongest.

They are the most **adaptable**.

And adaptation is born from one eternal decision:

To keep learning.

Not out of lack. But out of reverence for what still lies ahead.

The Story of Ishan, the Carpenter of Tides

In a fishing village that braved monsoons and memory, lived Ishan, a humble carpenter.

He had built boats for 40 years—boats that had carried generations through storms, trade, and celebration.

But the world began to change.

New fibreglass ships replaced wood.

Digital maps replaced starlit navigation.

Younger fishermen began mocking his "old ways."

His apprentice, Teerth, once asked, "Why don't you retire? You've already proven your worth."

Ishan smiled gently, placing his hand on a block of raw wood. "Because the tide never retires. And neither should the one who listens to it."

That week, Ishan enrolled in a marine engineering course online—at age 63. Not because he had fallen behind, but because he knew that **to stop learning was to start dying inwardly.**

Lifelong Learning as *Protection*

The world is uncertain.

Skills fade.

Industries dissolve.

Certainties become obsolete.

But the person who commits to constant renewal—who updates their thinking, unlearns old reflexes, and refines emotional and intellectual flexibility—**cannot be caught unprepared.**

Lifelong learning is your **intellectual immune system**.

It shields you from:

- Irrelevance
- Rigidity
- Resentment at change

Because you are not *anchored to a moment.*

You're *in rhythm* with evolution.

Like a tree that grows new rings even after storms, you learn not to resist the wind, but to **bend with wisdom**.

Lifelong Learning as *Propulsion*

Protection is only half the story.

Lifelong learning doesn't just *guard* your relevance—it *amplifies* your rise.

- The artist who learns new mediums mid-career unlocks new audiences.
- The leader who studies human psychology begins to inspire, not just instruct.
- The parent who reads about emotional intelligence builds deeper, healing bonds.
- The monk who explores modern science learns how to bridge worlds.

The mind that stays open becomes a **magnet for momentum**.
Because learning invites life to keep unfolding before you.

Learning Is Not a Classroom — It's a Posture

True lifelong learners are not addicted to certifications. They are devoted to **awareness**.

They learn from:

- Silence
- Nature
- Relationships
- Failure
- Children
- Adversity
- Questions that have no easy answers

Because they know:

Everything is a teacher when you are a humble student of reality.

Arup and the Library of Becoming

When Arup's retreat dissolved and his vision unravelled, what remained was not his résumé—it was his *receptivity*.

He read again—not to gather facts, but to remember essence.

He attended workshops—not to teach, but to feel like a beginner again.

He let his life become a library—not of books, but of **becomings**.

In that season, he learned:

- How to listen to people he once would have overlooked

- How to feel the world through poetry instead of process

- How to see failure as compost, not a coffin

And in that journey of learning, **his next life's chapter revealed itself—not as a return to success, but as an emergence into significance.**

The Deeper Truth

The world will outgrow every static identity you've worn.

But it will always make room for those who grow with it.

- A body that stretches remains agile.

- A mind that questions stays luminous.

- A soul that learns never ages.

You are not meant to be a monument.

You are meant to be a river—forever shaping, receiving, and giving.

Reflection

- What have you stopped being curious about that once lit your spirit?

- Where have you allowed pride to replace learning?

- What new horizon might open if you became a beginner again?

Commit not just to mastering life.

Commit to *meeting* it anew—every day, with every version of yourself that is yet to bloom.

Because in a world that worships performance, those who **honour transformation** are the ones who quietly shape the future.

Final Chapter

Becoming the Architect of Your Destiny

"True success isn't reaching a peak. It's realising the climb itself is home."

– Shree Shambav

Synopsis

Becoming the Architect of Your Destiny marks the turning point where philosophy meets embodiment. It is the moment where knowledge becomes structure, and structure becomes freedom. This section empowers the reader to reimagine their environment—not just physical, but emotional, relational, and spiritual—as a canvas upon which destiny is built daily. By curating relationships with purpose, crafting routines that serve vision, and aligning daily choices with long-term impact, the reader steps into authorship of their life. This is no longer about passive hope or unconscious repetition—it's about design, intention, and a rise that does not peak but evolves. In becoming the architect, one finally moves from survival to sovereignty.

The Architecture of Becoming—How Environment Shapes the Soul

The Silent Sculptor of Self

Every day, your surroundings whisper messages into your subconscious:

- The cluttered desk tells you to delay.
- The sterile room stifles your imagination.
- The noisy friend group applauds your distraction, not your growth.
- The dimly lit hallway of your home reminds you unconsciously: *nothing's changing.*

The environment is not just décor.

It is **direction**.

It shapes your micro-decisions, your self-belief, and eventually—your destiny.

We often try to change our lives through sheer willpower, forgetting this truth:

Willpower is a candle. The environment is the wind.

Niyara and the Window Garden

Niyara was a clinical psychologist who secretly wrote poetry at night.

Not for an audience—just for her own healing.

But years passed, and her poems remained in drawers.

Whenever she sat to write, something felt off. Distracted. Dry.

She blamed herself: "Maybe I'm not meant to be a writer."

Until one day, her mentor visited her flat in the city.

He walked in, looked around, and said nothing for several minutes. Then he asked:

"You say you want to write poems of light… but you live in shadows."

That sentence shook her.

He wasn't speaking metaphorically. Her desk faced a blank wall. Her chair was wobbly. The room was full of dusty psychology journals, not poetry. Her space honoured who she *had been*—not who she was becoming.

That evening, she did something radical.

She sold her old books.

Bought a desk made of reclaimed wood.

Painted the walls soft ochre.

Hung up quotes from different authors.

Moved her desk beside the window.

Planted a small vertical garden with jasmine and tulsi.

The first morning she sat there, she wrote four poems without trying. Not because she had changed—but because the *container* had.

She didn't need a new identity. She needed a new *environment that mirrored her inner voice.*

The Hidden Architecture of Behaviour

You think you decide your habits.

But much of what you do is simply a **response to your surroundings**.

- A bright, organised kitchen makes you eat differently than a cluttered one.

- A phone on your nightstand trains your nervous system for urgency, not serenity.

- A minimalist workspace calms your mental chatter more than any mindfulness app.

If the *external world is chaotic*, the *inner world follows suit.*

To design your environment is not aesthetic—

it is **psychological hygiene.**

Design Is an Act of Identity

Arup once said:

"Your space should not reflect where you are—it should speak to where you are going."

That's what he learned during his second reinvention.

After his retreat dissolved, and the world around him collapsed into ambiguity, he began redesigning his environment—**not with ambition, but with alignment**.

He moved to a simpler cottage near a river bend.

He arranged his books not by topic—but by how they made him *feel*.

He placed a copper diya near the entrance—not out of tradition, but to remind himself: "Light first. Always light first."

His writing nook overlooked wild grass, not a wall.

He created space not to **impress** the world—but to *invoke* something deeper within himself.

And slowly, his life moved in rhythm with his surroundings. He no longer had to *force* focus.

Stillness became the default.

Creativity returned without fanfare.

Practical Wisdom: Designing the Unseen Compass

You don't have to wait until everything collapses to redesign your life.

Start small. Ask:

- What does my workspace say about my dreams?
- Does my morning path support reflection or distraction?
- Is my bedroom a sanctuary—or a storage unit for stress?
- Do the people I allow near me nourish elevation or validation?

Remember:

Environment is more than space. It's systems. It's habits. It's who has your number. It's what surrounds your silence.

The most fulfilled people design **systems that protect their intention, surroundings that spark inspiration,** and **circles that challenge stagnation.**

The Inner Garden and the Outer Grove

Your mind is a garden.

But even the best seed won't bloom if the soil is toxic.

The same person, in a new environment, becomes a new person.

- A musician who moves to a city of sound suddenly rediscovers rhythm.
- A child with learning challenges blossoms in a classroom of kindness.
- A seeker in the right sangha finds answers without asking questions.

Change your environment, and your identity will evolve *organically*, not forcefully.

Reflection

- What parts of your environment reflect your past, not your future?
- What subtle shifts could be made to honour who you are becoming?
- What spaces need not be grand—but *sacred*?

You are not just the author of your life.

You are also the **architect**.

Design not just for function—but for *becoming*.

Because the shape of your space…

will shape the **story of your self**.

The Silent Architects — People as Portals of Destiny

"Some people come into your life as anchors. Others, as sails. You must know which is which before the storm hits."

The Unseen Tides of Influence

You are not walking your path alone.

You never were.

At every turn, visible or invisible, people shape your rhythm—

some as sacred accelerants,

others as subtle deterrents.

Not through grand betrayals or heroic sacrifices,

but through *presence*, through *energy*,

through the invisible **alignment—or is alignment—of their lives with your becoming**.

Often, it is not the lack of vision that stifles destiny,

but the weight of the wrong companions.

Your wings remember how to fly… only in skies where others are already airborne.

Leena and the Tapestry of Threads

Leena was a talented choreographer in a city addicted to cynicism. Her dance pieces told stories of grief, redemption, and resurrection—yet she found herself in circles where expression was mocked, ambition was dulled, and dreams were politely buried under banter and brunch.

Her friends were not bad people. They cared.

But they laughed when she said she wanted to take her art global.

"Leena, be realistic. You're lucky to even be booking gigs."

"Dance won't pay your bills. Just keep it a side thing."

"That festival you dream of is for insiders. It's rigged."

So, she shrank.

Not all at once.

But slowly, painfully.

Until her body could no longer move the way it used to. Not because she had aged—

but because she had internalised **stillness as safety**.

One day, she met a dancer from São Paulo named Marco. He wasn't famous. But he radiated something rare: conviction without ego.

He watched one of her pieces in an empty studio and said:

"You're hiding. Not your body—your fire."

That sentence was a mirror.

Within months, she applied for a residency abroad. Not because she believed she would get in—but because *he believed* she should try.

She was accepted.

And what followed wasn't just career elevation.

It was soul resurrection.

In that new circle of artists—purpose-driven, truth-seeking, fire-walking—her movement changed. Her stories deepened. Her body remembered its sacred ache.

She didn't need more talent. She needed more *alignment*.

The shift wasn't just who she was around.

It was what they *called forth* in her.

Relationship as Compass, Not Comfort

Most of us are told to surround ourselves with "good people." But the truth is—good isn't enough.

You must ask:

- *Do they reflect the life I'm building?*
- *Do they challenge my shadows without shaming my light?*

- *Do they pull me deeper into alignment—or comfort me in dissonance?*

Anchors don't always feel heavy at first.

Sometimes they feel like home—because they mirror your old self.

But not all that feels familiar is aligned with your future.

True alignment whispers: "I see your highest. Let's rise there together."

The Compass of Arup

Arup learned this not once, but many times.

In the rise of his retreat, he was surrounded by visionaries and architects of truth.

But during its fall—some old ties returned. Familiar voices. Comfort circles.

The kind who said: *"Maybe it's time to settle."*

"You've done enough."

At first, he leaned in—out of exhaustion, not clarity.

But one evening, in a circle of fire-walkers—sages, artists, thinkers—he shared his grief. Not his plan. Not his brand. Just his raw, unvarnished heart.

They didn't console him.

One woman said:

"You're not here to resurrect what collapsed. You're here to rise from it."

Another said:

"We didn't gather to fix you. We gathered to remind you—what still lives inside you."

That night, he remembered:

Your tribe is not who soothes your wounds.

It's who speaks to your medicine.

The Physics of Alignment

Just as sound needs the right medium to travel,

purpose needs the right *people* to propagate.

You could be a symphony—

but if you're surrounded by silence, your notes dissolve.

Surround yourself with:

- Those who **stretch your standards**, not shrink your goals.
- Those who **celebrate your stillness**, not mistake it for stagnation.
- Those who **challenge your ego**, not coddle your comfort.

Because **destiny is not just direction—it's also atmosphere.**

Reflection: Who Holds Your Becoming?

- Who are the five people you speak to most?
- What do their lives whisper to your soul?
- Are they pulling you upward—or anchoring you in repetition?

And more crucially:

- Do *you* bring that same oxygen to others?

You are both seed and soil in this life. Choose your garden carefully.

Because some people will water your roots.

Others will step on your shoots.

And a rare few—will grow with you under the same rising sun.

From Drift to Design — Becoming the Architect of the Unseen

"Life does not ask if you are ready. It simply moves.

You either build your sail—or get dragged by the tide."

The Unlived Life

Many live as if life is something that *happens* to them.

Like weather.

Or traffic.

Days unfold not by intention, but by notification.

We respond to emails, deadlines, emergencies, and emotions—

Like a dancer with no music, waiting to be pulled by someone else's rhythm.

This is the realm of the **reactive self**.

- Life becomes a series of responses.
- Choices are disguised as obligations.
- Time is governed by external fires.
- The future is shaped by today's noise—not tomorrow's clarity.

In this state, you are not living—you are surviving.

Dev and the Unwritten Script

Dev was a mid-level executive at a multinational firm.

Good paycheck. Good performance.

But every day, he woke up with a tightness in his chest. A quiet voice whispering,

"This is not it."

He drowned it with discipline. Gym. Goals. Gratitude journals.

But it wasn't until he missed his daughter's school play—for the third year in a row—that something cracked.

That night, sitting in the dim light of his study, Dev found an old sketchpad.

He had once dreamed of being an architect.

Not just of buildings—but of *experiences*.

Of **spaces that healed, inspired, and invited beauty.**

He ran his hand over the dusty pages. The designs were still there.

So was the dream.

And that's when the question arose—not from guilt, but from deep knowing:

"If I do not *create* the life I want—who will?"

Designing in the Dark

We often think clarity must precede action. But the truth is—**creation is what clears the fog**.

Like a sculptor who chisels with no final shape in mind, **life design begins with courage, not certainty.**

Dev didn't quit his job the next day.

He began waking up an hour earlier—not to respond to emails, but to design a healing pavilion inspired by Indian temple courtyards.

He started volunteering with a local NGO building schools in rural areas.

He didn't escape his old life.

He *rewrote it*, brick by brick.

From Reactor to Creator: The Shift

The difference between the **reactive** and the **deliberate** life lies in five sacred shifts:

1. **From Schedule to Sacred Space**

Reactive: "What's on my calendar today?"

Intentional: "What inner state will I cultivate today?"

2. **From External Control to Inner Compass**

Reactive: "What's urgent?"

Intentional: "What's important—even if no one else sees it?"

3. **From Fear of Uncertainty to Dialogue with It**

Reactive: Avoid discomfort.

Intentional: Engage it as a sculptor engages raw stone.

4. **From Passive Waiting to Active Choosing**

Reactive: Hope for change.

Intentional: *Be* the change agent.

5. **From Consuming Life to Composing It**

Reactive: Scroll, react, repeat.

Intentional: Create, choose, renew.

The Compass of Arup

Arup, too, had once been a master of reaction.

Board meetings. Book deals. Podcasts. Panels.

But there came a point where his days were full—yet his soul was famished.

When his retreat began to dissolve, it would've been easy to react: more marketing, more networking, more hustle.

Instead, he paused. Sat by the stream behind Aprameya Hall.

And asked the question that changed everything:

"What wants to be born through me—*now*—not as I was, but as I have become?"

From that moment, his life wasn't a product of planning. It became a **living ritual of listening, alignment, and conscious crafting**.

Not because things became certain.

But because *he stopped waiting for certainty, to started living deliberately.*

The Architecture of Becoming

Think of your life as a **sacred house**.

- **Reactive living** is like inheriting a house you never chose, rearranging the furniture endlessly, but never asking if you want to live there.

- **Deliberate living** is when you pick up the hammer, the blueprint, the light—

- and begin *building* room by room, even if all you have at first is one beam and a prayer.

You design not just your goals—

but your mornings.

Your conversations.

Your environment.

Your inner narrative.

You become the architect—*not* of outcomes, but of essence.

From Noise to Narrative

If life feels chaotic—ask:

- What have I been *responding* to?
- Where have I outsourced authorship of my own story?
- What one small thing can I *create* today—not for applause, but for alignment?

And then, write the first sentence of a life that feels like home.

Because ultimately:

You are not here to live by default.

You are here to write the story only you were born to tell.

The Rise That Never Ends

"Some mountains aren't meant to be conquered—only circled, slowly, reverently, year after year, so their wisdom seeps into your bones."

The Myth of Arrival

We are conditioned to believe that life is a ladder:

- You rise.
- You arrive.
- You stay.

This myth seduces us into chasing peaks—titles, wealth, applause, enlightenment—believing that once we reach *that one summit*, we will be safe, fulfilled, whole.

But real life has its own language.

It speaks in seasons, spirals, and silence.

The truth?

There is no final rise. Only unfolding. Only becoming.

Even the stars, ancient as they are, are still expanding.

Amara and the Fire That Dims

Amara was a renowned poet-sage in her fifties.

She had written books that stirred revolutions, spoken on stages that echoed her name across continents.

And yet, one winter, she found herself weeping over a sink of unwashed dishes.

Her words had stopped coming.

For months, she tried to "rise" again. Meditation retreats. Writing residencies. Herbal tonics.

But her spark had gone quiet.

Until one dusk, while visiting a quiet Himalayan monastery, she met a monk who had once been a calligrapher.

They sat in silence for an hour before she finally asked:

"Do you ever feel like you've lost what made you... *you*?"

The monk smiled.

"The river does not lose its way when it flows underground.

It simply changes form.

The rise never ends—it just sometimes wears different clothes."

Something cracked open in her.

That evening, she picked up a broom and began sweeping the temple floor—not to find her spark again, but to honour where she was.

She began *living* her poetry, not writing it.

Serving tea became her stanza. Silence, her metaphor.

And slowly, without demand or drama—her fire returned.

Not as lightning this time, but as warm embers.

Not for applause, but for presence.

That's when she realised:

The rise never stopped. She had just changed altitudes.

The Anatomy of the Endless Rise

To live a rise that never ends means to understand **growth not as a goal, but as a vow**.

It is a choice to keep becoming—regardless of circumstance, age, or recognition.

Let us explore its **three sacred dimensions**:

1. Spiritual: The Soul's Slow Unfolding

This is not about doing more.

It is about *remembering more deeply* who you are beneath the noise.

Like a tree whose roots grow deeper even when no leaves appear, your inner rise is often invisible.

It is marked by:

- Learning to sit with discomfort without fleeing.
- Surrendering identity to become more essence.
- Seeking less of "what's next?" and more of "what's now?"

True elevation is not performance. It is **presence**.

2. Emotional: The Art of Renewal

A sustained rise requires emotional resilience—not through suppression, but through *integration*.

You don't climb forever without pausing, exhaling, grieving.

- Cry when needed.
- Retreat when called.
- Rewrite the narrative without shame.

Every rise includes a fall inward.

The caterpillar dissolves completely before becoming a butterfly. That dissolution is not failure. It is *alchemy*.

3. Practical: Rhythms Over Rallies

A rise that never ends isn't powered by adrenaline—but by **rituals**.

The most evolved souls are not frantic—they are rhythmic:

- Morning stillness.
- Evening reflection.
- Weekly soul dates.
- Seasonal reinvention.

They build systems that serve their *state*, not just their status.

Because what sustains elevation is not effort—it is **alignment**.

Arup and the Mountain That Grew With Him

Arup, once praised for his visionary rise in both art and enterprise, eventually stepped away—not to stop rising, but to rise **inward**.

Years later, people would ask:

"How did you stay relevant?"

"How did you not burn out?"

He would laugh, gently.

"I stopped trying to rise in one direction. I let the mountain grow *with me.*"

In Shambav Hall, he would often light a single lamp and sit with seekers in a circle—not as their guide, but as a fellow pilgrim.

He would speak of the **Rise That Never Ends** as:

- A practice of listening more than leading.
- A reverence for slowness in a fast world.
- A return to the sacred ordinary.

He taught not from the summit—but from the spiral path, where he was still walking.

The Invitation

A rise that never ends is not found in:

- Crushing goals.
- Chasing peak states.
- Comparing timelines.

It is found in:

- Recommitting to your soul's calling, even after silence.
- Rising in the dark, with no applause.
- Elevating others as part of your rise.

Because ultimately:

To rise endlessly is to love endlessly.

To learn endlessly.

To let go endlessly.

To live not for the height—but for the depth.

Whisper

You do not have to reach a mountaintop to be rising.

*You only have to be **becoming**, again and again.*

And when your rise aligns with love—not achievement—
It sustains itself.
Like the moon.
Like breath.
Like spirit.

WRAP UP

Rise, and Keep Rising

"Power without direction is chaos. Riches without meaning are noise. Only aligned wealth sings."

— Shree Shambav

Synopsis

Rise, and Keep Rising is the final call—an invitation to embrace the total integration of power, riches, and wealth, not as trophies, but as tools for living a deeply meaningful life. This section transcends frameworks and tactics, urging the reader to reflect on how far they've come and what still calls to be born through them. It is about harmonising influence with humility, abundance with purpose, and freedom with service. The journey doesn't end here—it evolves. With clarity, mindset, and alignment now in place, the future becomes a blank canvas. The question is no longer whether you will rise—but how boldly you will write what comes next.

The Triad of True Prosperity

"Power without purpose becomes tyranny.

Wealth without meaning becomes a burden.

But when soul meets strategy, and impact meets intention—

A new kind of richness is born: one that nourishes not only the life we live, but the lives we touch."

The Mirage of More

The world is filled with people chasing one corner of the triangle:

- **Power**: Influence, control, reach, command.
- **Riches**: Currency, assets, possessions, status.
- **Wealth**: Security, legacy, abundance, options.

Each of these, when pursued alone, has a shadow:

- Power without soul corrupts.
- Riches without rhythm suffocate.
- Wealth without wisdom becomes a hollow inheritance.

We've seen empires rise on sheer might, only to collapse from inner emptiness.

We've seen millionaires numb in their mansions, disconnected from joy or meaning.

We've seen visionary voices silenced by systems that never gave them structure.

But when **meaning becomes the unifying current**—when power, riches, and wealth are not the destination, but the **servants of purpose**—a deeper alchemy unfolds.

Let us explore that alchemy.

Elian: The Architect of Wholeness

Elian was a strategist.

In his early years, he was hungry—not for money, but for movement. For impact. For victory.

He built brands that conquered industries.

He advised governments.

He commanded rooms with ease.

Yet after a decade, he sat alone in his glass-walled apartment overlooking the city skyline and felt… hollow.

His power made others move.

His riches bought him everything.

His wealth gave him choices.

But none of it **centred** him.

Until one evening, in a remote desert town, he met a woman named Isha who ran a solar school for girls.

They had dinner by firelight. No lights, no logos.

She asked him one question:

"Elian, your work moves people. But does it move *you*?"

He couldn't answer.

So he stayed. For three months. In silence.

He taught the girls how to build frameworks.

They taught him how to build a fire with no matches.

He returned a different man.

Back in the city, he still did business—but he redesigned every system.

- His investments now backed regenerative projects.
- His boardroom began with moments of stillness.
- His life no longer chased impact metrics—it *became* one.

And with that inner alignment, his reach grew.

Not because he sought more, but because he **became more**.

The Triad Explained: A New Geometry of Greatness

Power (Action, Voice, Influence)

Power is not about domination.

It is about **direction**.

When tethered to purpose:

- Power becomes stewardship, not control.
- It amplifies truth, not ego.
- It protects the vulnerable instead of exploiting them.

Like the river that carves mountains—not by brute force, but by patient flow—**purposeful power is quiet yet unstoppable.**

Riches (Currency, Flow, Fuel)

Money is not evil. Nor is it holy.

It is simply **neutral energy**—it becomes what we program into it.

Aligned with meaning, riches:

- Fuel art, healing, and education.
- Restore ecosystems.
- Break cycles of generational poverty.

We don't need less money—we need **more conscious stewards of it.**

In the right hands, a dollar can become a revolution.

Wealth (Time, Choice, Legacy)

Wealth is not just financial—it is **spiritual spaciousness**.

To be wealthy is to:

- Choose rest without guilt.

- Give without depletion.
- Walk through life without begging for permission.

True wealth allows you to say **yes** to your soul's voice, not just the world's noise.

And when built with meaning, your wealth does not end with you—it becomes **a song your descendants continue singing**.

Arup and the Golden Triad

Years after his own renaissance in Aprameya Hall, Arup was once asked on a podcast:

"You've built power, acquired riches, and established wealth. But you seem more peaceful now than ever. What changed?"

He paused and said:

"I stopped chasing each one separately.

I let meaning braid them together.

Now, they serve something bigger than me."

His new ventures were slower but deeper.

He mentored not for influence, but to **transfer fire**.

His wealth built sanctuaries of silence and stories.

And in that alignment, everything expanded—not through hustle, but through harmony.

The Invitation to You

If you're chasing riches—ask: *For what higher cause?*

If you're craving power—ask: *Whose life will I elevate with it?*

If you're building wealth—ask: *Will it free me and others, or trap us in golden cages?*

When all three serve your **deepest why**, they become:

- Fire that ignites movements.
- Water that nourishes future roots.
- Earth that holds your legacy gently.

This is how a life becomes **extraordinary**—not by stacking trophies, but by **synchronising soul and structure**.

Whisper

You were never meant to choose between power, riches, or wealth.

You were meant to **unite them through purpose**.

Let meaning be your gravity.

Let your soul be the architect.

And watch how your influence expands—not like a wildfire, but like **a sacred rhythm that echoes across generations**.

The Quiet Grace of Greatness

"The moon holds the power to stir oceans, yet it remains still in the sky.

True influence does not roar. It radiates."

The Seduction of Success

Influence.

Freedom.

Impact.

Three of the most coveted forces in today's world.

Each glittering with promise, each wrapped in illusion.

We chase them with the hope that they will complete us.

- **Influence**, because we want to be heard.
- **Freedom**, because we want to be unbound.
- **Impact**, because we want to matter.

And yet—how many of us, in chasing these very things, lose the one thing that can never be replaced?

Our peace. Our presence. Our soul.

Mia: The Song That Lost Its Singer

Mia was a global changemaker.

By 32, she had spoken on international stages, led multiple non-profits, and had over a million followers across platforms.

She was a voice for the voiceless.

An advocate for those in pain.

A symbol of strength.

And yet, one evening after a powerful keynote in Amsterdam, she returned to her hotel room, removed her heels, sat on the floor—and wept.

Not from sadness.

From **exhaustion**.

She had become a lighthouse for others, but forgot to keep her own flame tended.

She realised she had **influence**, but no intimacy.

Freedom, but no stillness.

Impact, but no joy.

In her pursuit to change the world, she had forgotten to *feel* the world.

So she disappeared from public life.

No explanation. No farewell tour.

She moved to a coastal village in Portugal.

She walked barefoot. She painted.

She sat in silence. She listened to birdsong more than applause.

And in that stillness, she found something deeper than success:

Surrender. Simplicity. Soulful rhythm.

Eventually, Mia returned—not to the stage, but to sacred circles.

Her words now carried the weight of wisdom, not just wins.

Her influence no longer demanded the spotlight.

It *invited silence.*

Her freedom was not in flights and schedules—it was in choosing when to say **no**.

Her impact was no longer viral—it was **visceral**.

The Trap of Misaligned Success

In our world, success is often measured by:

- How many followers.
- How much financial independence.
- How many lives have you've touched.

But if these achievements pull you away from your essence—are they truly yours? Or have you become **a servant to your own shine**?

Many powerful people wake up one day to find:

- Their **influence** is performative.
- Their **freedom** is chaotic.
- Their **impact** is unsustainable.

Because the soul was never meant to carry **eternal expansion** without **deep rooting**.

Harmony: A Different Definition of Greatness

To live in harmony with influence, freedom, and impact means:

- **You don't chase them. You channel them.**
- **You don't flaunt them. You *flow* with them.**
- **You don't measure them. You *embody* them.**

It's a quiet, internal architecture.

Like a tree:

- Your **influence** is in the shade you give, not the height you boast.
- Your **freedom** is in your rootedness, not just in wandering winds.
- Your **impact** is in how deeply your presence alters the soil, the sky, and the spirit of others.

Arup: The Monk Behind the Marketplace

After Arup's rebirth at the Temple of the Unseen Flame, he no longer sought virality or valuation.

He still ran projects.

Still mentored leaders.

Still moved resources to where they were most needed.

But now, **his rhythm had changed.**

He began each day not with metrics, but meditation.

When people asked:

"How do you manage so much and stay so peaceful?"

He would smile and say:

"I don't manage. I align. I let go of what wants to rush. I hold what wants to root."

Arup's **influence** came through a still presence.

His **freedom** through disciplined surrender.

His **impact** is through authentic intimacy.

He became a man not consumed by his reach, but anchored in his return.

Your Reflection: Are You Building a Kingdom or a Cage?

Take a breath.

Ask:

- Is your influence deep or just wide?
- Is your freedom real or reactive?

- Is your impact sustainable—or does it drain you?

If you want to build a life that endures beyond performance, begin with this:

- **Anchor before you ascend.**
- **Root before you radiate.**
- **Feel before you fix.**

Your greatness does not require grandiosity.

It requires **grounding**.

Whisper

Let your life be like a sacred river.

Let influence flow gently, nourishing all it touches.

Let freedom be the bend that honours the landscape.

Let impact be the quiet depth that changes everything—without noise, without need.

This is harmony.

This is grace.

This is how you rise—and never burn.

The Door You Didn't Know You Closed

"It's not always the mountain that holds us back.

Sometimes, it's the stone in our shoe."

The Invisible Cage

Many of us live like birds in open cages.

The door is not locked.

The sky is near.

The winds call.

But still—we do not fly.

Why?

Not because we can't.

But because we carry **invisible barriers**—old, hidden, often unnamed—that feel like safety, but act like shackles.

These barriers are not made of iron.

They are made of *unhealed stories, subtle fears, unquestioned beliefs,* and *outdated identities.*

- A childhood moment where you were told, "Don't be too much."
- A silent decision after heartbreak: "I won't open fully again."
- An inherited belief: "People like us don't live lives like that."

Each of these becomes a thread in the **web of inner limits**—a soft prison made of your own forgotten agreements.

Arup and the Locked Gate

After his return from the Temple of the Unseen Flame, Arup felt lighter, wiser, quieter.

But something still tugged.

Every time a new opportunity came—a call to speak, to lead, to love more deeply—he would hesitate.

Not out of fear.

Out of a strange sense of unworthiness, a whisper in his bones:

"Haven't you already failed once? Don't fly too high this time."

One morning, he sat at the old wooden gate that led to a mist-covered valley behind the retreat. The gate hadn't been opened in years. It groaned with rust, vines weaving through its slats.

He had always thought it was locked.

But as he placed his hand on it—gently—it creaked open with a low sigh.

Not locked. Never was.

Just *neglected*.

Just *assumed shut*.

He stepped through. The air changed. The view widened. And something inside him finally exhaled.

"What else in me," he wondered, "have I left closed—not because it was locked, but because I never tried to turn the handle?"

That day, he didn't scale a new summit.

He simply *re-entered a room in himself that he had long abandoned.*

And that changed everything.

Identifying Your Invisible Barriers

Here are some of the subtle forms they take:

1. **Inner Language:**

Listen to how you speak to yourself.

- "I should be grateful for what I have."
- "It's too late to start over."
- "Who am I to dream that big?"

These phrases may seem wise, but often hide fear dressed as humility.

2. **Repeated Patterns:**

Notice what keeps happening.

- Do you always pull back at the brink of success?
- Do you attract similar relationships, bosses, betrayals?

These are not coincidences—they are mirrors of unresolved truths.

3. **Emotional Numbness:**

Sometimes the barrier is not pain—but the refusal to feel anything at all.

Numbness is a signal. Not of peace, but of disconnection.

4. **Unseen Loyalties:**

You may be unconsciously loyal to your past, your family's limitations, or your culture's definition of success.

- "If I become too successful, will I still belong?"
- "Will my rise dishonour those who never got the chance?"

These inner contracts are invisible—but binding.

From Self-Awareness to Integration

Becoming aware of these barriers is only step one.

True transformation begins when you **integrate** the wounded parts, the protective identities, the unseen fears—and offer them new roles.

- Let your inner critic become your inner editor—wise, but not cruel.

- Let your fear of failure become your compass for courage.

- Let your past pain become the soil from which empathy blooms.

Integration means: *Nothing is rejected. Everything is alchemised.*

The Shadow Garden

Imagine your soul as a garden.

Some areas bloom with colour.

Others lie in shadow, overgrown, ignored.

Those shadowed places are not dead.

They are simply waiting.

You must walk there.

Not to judge.

But to listen. To learn. To *replant*.

The parts of you you've buried are often the **keys to your next rise.**

But only if you're willing to **go there.**

The Gentle Inventory: Questions to Uncover the Unseen

1. What belief about myself do I keep accepting without proof?

2. What am I afraid would happen if I truly succeeded?

3. Whose voice is still guiding my decisions—though they are no longer present?

4. When did I stop trusting myself—and why?

Ask.

Wait.

Listen.

Not for answers in words—but for sensations, memories, and gentle recognitions.

Whisper: The Sky You Forgot You Belong To

The rise you seek is not on the other side of more hustle.

It is waiting inside the room you locked long ago.

But here's the truth:

- The gate isn't locked.
- The door isn't sealed.
- The barrier isn't real—it's remembered.

And the moment you see that clearly, the weight begins to lift.

Like Arup, may you walk barefoot through your own forgotten gardens.

May you push gently on the doors you assumed were closed. And may you remember:

You were never broken—only buried.

You were never lost—only layered.

And your next rise is not about becoming more…

but about becoming whole.

The Pen in the Fire

"The past may write your prologue, but only presence writes your power."

— From the journal of Arup, written on the night he stopped blaming fate.

The Story of Arup and the Burnt Pages

After his quiet return from years of building and breaking, Arup sat alone one evening in the upper chamber of Aprameya Hall.

The room was simple—wooden floors, earthen walls, and an open window facing the hills. There was no noise but the crackle of fire, and the ticking of a clock whose hands seemed unsure whether they moved forward or simply circled back again and again.

In front of him lay a box of old journals—some stained with rain, others covered in dust. They held his earliest ambitions, the dreams of a younger man: outlines of the perfect retreat, detailed goals, quarterly forecasts, lists of people he wanted to impress.

He read them with tenderness, but also unease.

So much of his life, he realised, had been authored by **reaction**:

Reacting to approval or rejection.

Reacting to what others were building.

Reacting to fear disguised as ambition.

Reacting to his own wounds disguised as goals.

He had written many chapters—but they weren't always his voice.

Sometimes it was the voice of fear.

Other times, the echo of inherited definitions of success.

Occasionally, the quiet manipulations of unmet needs.

Arup stood, took a matchstick, and gently lit one of the pages.

Not in anger.

In *release*.

Not to destroy the story, but to *purify* the author.

And that night, for the first time in years, he sat by candlelight—not to rewrite the past, but to finally write the **true next chapter**, with a clear hand.

The Myth of Control vs. the Power of Authorship

Authorship does not mean controlling every plot twist.

Life will still offer surprise chapters. Tragedy. Change. Conflict.

But authorship means this:

- **You choose how you frame what happens.**
- **You choose what you create next, not just what you respond to.**
- **You decide which part of you will hold the pen: the wounded self, the wise self, or the awakened self.**

There's a difference between living by default and living by design.

One is like sleepwalking through a script handed to you.

The other is like becoming a conscious co-creator—with Life, Spirit, and Self.

Mentally: Reclaiming the Narrator's Chair

True authorship begins in the **mind**—where you rewrite internal narratives.

Instead of:

- "This always happens to me." →

You begin asking, "What is life asking *from* me through this?"

Instead of:

- "I'm stuck here." →

You wonder, "What is seeking to emerge *through* me here?"

The mental shift is subtle but seismic.

You move from being a **character in someone else's plot** to the **narrator of your own mythos**.

Emotionally: Healing the Inner Editor

Every author wrestles with an editor.

But in life, that editor is often your **inner child's fear of rejection**, or the **inner critic's obsession with perfection**.

To author your life, emotionally, you must:

- Let grief teach you, not trap you.
- Let anger pass through—not own the pen.
- Let joy be a guide, not a reward.
- Let shame be seen, then set down.

Arup had once said, "The moment I stopped hiding parts of me, my writing became more true—and so did my life."

Emotional authorship means wholeness.

It's not about controlling emotion—it's about integrating it.

So every chapter is *honest, alive, fully felt*—and yet *clearly chosen.*

Spiritually: Writing with the Flame, not the Finger

You don't write a sacred life with willpower alone.

You write it with **alignment**.

- With your deeper calling.
- With the truth of your soul, not the trends of the moment.
- With surrender to a Source greater than your ego.

Spiritually, authorship asks you to ask:

"Am I writing to impress, or to express the divine within me?"

A life authored from the soul has a rhythm that outlasts seasons.

It is not always fast, but it is **eternally resonant**.

The Compass, The Chisel, and The Flame

- **The Mind is your Compass.** It sets the direction.
- **The Heart is your Chisel.** It shapes each moment with care and emotion.

- **The Soul is your Flame.** It ensures that what you write has light—not just lines.

To live a well-authored life, you must **align all three.**

The Journal Entry: From Reaction to Creation

If you feel lost, begin with a question Arup once used when he forgot who he was:

"What would the future-me thank me for doing today?"

And then...

- Write one page each morning—*not of what you must do*, but *of who you choose to be.*
- End each day with a line of gratitude—not for what went right, but for what grew within you.

In time, your life will no longer be a series of reactions.

It will become a **living manuscript**—a soul's legacy etched not in stone, but in the choices you made when no one was watching.

The Final Note: You Are The Author

Dear Seeker,

There will always be storms.

There will always be critics—some outside, many within.

There will always be edits.

But never forget this:

The pen is still in your hand.

The page is still unwritten.

The fire within is still warm.

Write not for applause.

Write not for revenge.

Write not from fear.

Write because you are awake.

Write because your soul remembers.

Write because the next chapter deserves your voice.

Let your life be literature.

Let your choices be poetry.

Let your presence be the sacred punctuation between fate and freedom.

APPENDICES

APPENDICES A

Actionable Insights & Tools

"Living the Rise: Sacred Tools for Daily Mastery and Lifelong Becoming"

"Insight without embodiment is a dream.

But insight made daily, tracked gently, and honoured fully—

becomes the architecture of destiny."

— From Arup's journal

I. The Soul Compass: Daily Alignment Tracker

This is not a habit tracker. This is a *soul integrator*—a tool to help you start each day not by checking boxes but by aligning your internal compass before action.

Morning Prompts (The Rise of Intention)

- What is the one value I want to embody today?
- What is mine to do—not from urgency, but from purpose?
- Who can I support or uplift today with truth or presence?

- What truth do I need to remember, even if the world forgets it?

Evening Reflections (The Return to Self)

- Did I move from vision or reaction?
- Where did I abandon myself today? Where did I return?
- What one small act felt aligned with my future self?
- What am I grateful for—not because it was easy, but because it grew me?

A space to write your "Soul Score" (0–10)

Not for judgment—but to build emotional honesty, not just productivity.

II. The Environment Audit: Designing Sacred Spaces

"We don't just build environments. They build us."

— Arup, during his retreat reconstruction

This worksheet invites you to examine your **physical, digital, and relational environments**.

Categories to Reflect and Redesign

1. **Physical Space:**
    - Does my home/office reflect my values or my past conditioning?

- What 3 objects energise me? What 3 deplete me?

2. **Digital Landscape:**
    - Are the first 30 minutes of my screen time intentional or inherited?
    - Whose voices dominate my feed? Do they reflect who I'm becoming?

3. **Social Circle Audit:**
    - Who stretches me spiritually?
    - Who mirrors my mediocrity?
    - Who drains versus replenishes?

Use the "Let Go / Lean In" grid to start designing the space that breathes your becoming.

III. The Circle of Surrender & Strength: Emotional Integration Exercise

Inspired by Arup's letting go beneath the fallen Peepal tree, this guided worksheet walks you through transforming collapse into clarity.

Exercise Flow

- What is collapsing in my life right now (structure, identity, relationship)?
- What story am I telling about this collapse?

- What deeper truth is being revealed beneath this collapse?

- What strength can only be born through my surrender?

Ritual:

Burn or bury an object representing your "old chapter."

Write a letter from your future self thanking you for letting go.

IV. Life Authorship Framework: Crafting the Next Chapter

This framework mirrors the core philosophy of the book: transitioning from reacting to designing.

The Four Levels of Life Design

1. **Mental:** What dominant beliefs are scripting my decisions?

2. **Emotional:** Where do I still react from unintegrated wounds?

3. **Spiritual:** What is the essence I'm meant to transmit through my existence?

4. **Practical:** What is one aligned decision I can make this week?

Use this framework quarterly to realign your path.

Integration Question:
"If my life were a book, would the next chapter be authored by my fear, my ego, or my soul?"

V. The Rhythm of Resilience: The 7-Day Reset Ritual

A mini-retreat structure you can implement anytime you feel lost, off-course, or weary.

Daily Structure Overview

- **Day 1:** *Silence* – No external input. Just you, a journal, and stillness.

- **Day 2:** *Release* – Write down and physically discard what no longer serves.

- **Day 3:** *Reclaim* – Declare your values. Remember your why.

- **Day 4:** *Redesign* – Audit your space, time, and connections.

- **Day 5:** *Recommit* – Choose one habit and one soul ritual to restart.

- **Day 6:** *Reignite* – Do something courageous (call, create, confess).

- **Day 7:** *Rest and Receive* – Let insight rise. Let joy be enough.

Reflection Prompt Each Day:

"What part of me is being born again?"

VI. The Inner Circle Blueprint: Mapping Purposeful Relationships

Purpose does not thrive in isolation. This worksheet helps you intentionally build your **circle of destiny accelerators**—not just friends, but fellow flame-keepers.

Roles to Identify

- **The Mirror:** Who reflects your blind spots with love?
- **The Architect:** Who helps you see the bigger blueprint?
- **The Anchor:** Who holds space when you forget your strength?
- **The Flame:** Who reignites your joy, purpose, and creative fire?

Map them. Reach out. Or call them in through prayer and presence.

VII. The Eternal Rise Manifesto (Printable)

**I rise, not to escape what was,
but to embody what is becoming.**

I choose to begin again—

not because I failed,

but because I remember I'm still unfolding.

I do not chase. I align.

I do not prove. I express.

I do not conquer. I tend.

This rise has no peak—

only deepening.

Only awakening.

Only a return

to who I have always been.

— *Author Your Becoming*

Life Coach and Philanthropist

Shree Shambav is the visionary founder of the Shree Shambav Ayur Rakshita Foundation (www.shambav-ayurrakshita.org). He founded this institution with a lofty goal: to recognise human identity across gender, ethnicity, and nationality. Through this organisation, he wants to assist all communities in realising their full potential and the intrinsic beauty of life.

Shree Shambav, a Life Coach, is dedicated to supporting people on their journeys of self-discovery and empowerment. He assists people in discovering who they are, determining what inspires and drives them, and overcoming limiting ideas. His approach clarifies what one wants in life, assisting people through goal-setting and a step-by-step process for achieving them. He empowers people to make deliberate and responsible decisions, allowing them to identify their blind spots and evolve as individuals via the use of numerous strategies and tools.

The foundation's bold, uncompromising, and compassionate ventures are always aimed at initiating the "Inner Transformation" process. They focus on spiritual growth, personal growth, and self-healing while emphasising that true progress lies in "Inclusive Growth and Co-existence." This philosophy drives all their initiatives, encouraging a holistic approach to development and well-being.

Under Shree Shambav's leadership, the foundation has launched several impactful movements:

Shree Shambav Green Movement: This mission is to create a healthy, green, and clean earth through responsible water conservation and greening initiatives. The movement strives to make the world a green paradise by encouraging sustainable living and environmental responsibility.

Shree Shambav Vidya Vedhika (Vizhuthugal): This project aims to help students and children by offering training, books, stationery, and uniforms. It aims to provide the next generation with the tools and resources they need to excel both academically and personally.

Shree Shambav and his foundation exemplify the spirit of compassion, transformation, and inclusive growth via their work, which has a profound impact on individuals and communities around the world. His work exemplifies the power of acknowledging and nourishing the human spirit, creating a world in which everyone can reach their full potential and appreciate the beauty of life.

TESTIMONIALS

Journey of Soul - Karma - "We die in our twenties and are buried at eighty." Remember that nothing can stop someone who refuses to be stopped. "Most people do not fail; they simply give up." Shree Shambav deserves full credit. It allowed me to sit and consider what I might miss out on in life. The author has delved into every aspect of our daily lives. How can a seemingly insignificant change in these seemingly insignificant details bring us such joy? The Soul of Journey teaches you the "art of living" as well as the "art of dying."

Twenty + One Series - The rich cultural heritage offered a host in twenty + one short stories with incredible imagination, morals and values prevalent at a given time, influencing how people respond to a crisis or any situation. The author has recreated images with universal values and morals. The plentiful of fascinating from faraway lands would leave the modern play and story writers a cringe. The book supports trust and immeasurable values instilling hope for the new generations.

Death - "Shree Shambav's 'Death - Light of Life and the Shadow of Death' is an extraordinary masterpiece that delves deep into the profound questions surrounding our existence and mortality. The book's opening statement, 'Nothing ever truly dies; it simply ceases to exist in one form before resuming it in another,' sets the stage for a thought-provoking exploration of death's multifaceted nature. Shambav's remarkable ability to navigate the philosophical complexities of death and our universal fear of it is both enlightening and comforting. This book is a testament to the power of understanding and acceptance."

Whispers of Eternity - "Reading 'Whispers of Eternity' by Shree Shambav was a transformative experience that left me captivated from beginning to end. Each section of this exquisite collection delves into the myriad facets of existence, offering poignant reflections on life, death, and everything in between. Shree Shambav's verses are a testament to the beauty of language and the power of expression, inviting readers to embark on a journey of self-discovery and spiritual awakening. Whether celebrating life's simple joys or grappling with the complexities of human emotion, this book is a timeless companion that speaks to the heart and soul of every reader."

Life Changing Journey Series - "Life Changing Journey Series II Inspirational Quotes" is a remarkable collection that illuminates the path to self-discovery and personal growth. With its inspiring quotes and insightful reflections, this book serves as a beacon of light in a world often shrouded in darkness. Each quote offers wisdom, guidance, and encouragement, reminding readers of their inner strength and resilience. A must-read for anyone seeking inspiration and enlightenment.

Learn To Love Yourself – "A Heartfelt Guide to Authentic Self-Love." "Learn to Love Yourself" invites readers on a transformative journey to embrace their true essence in a world often focused on external validation. Through ten insightful chapters, it gently reveals principles of genuine self-love, guiding readers to deepen their connection with themselves. Beyond surface positivity, it encourages the cultivation of resilient self-acceptance, from embracing one's unique qualities to setting empowering boundaries. With inspiring stories and practical wisdom, this book is a trusted companion on the path to inner peace, fulfilment, and joy, helping readers build lives that reflect their authentic selves.

The Power of Letting Go – This book has been a gift to my spiritual journey. Shree Shambav's insights into attachment, personal growth cycles, and forgiveness are enlightening. The concept of seven-year cycles resonated with me, helping me understand the natural phases of life. I feel more empowered to let go of what no longer serves me and step into a life of freedom and fulfilment. A truly beautiful read!

A Journey of Lasting Peace – "A Journey of Lasting Peace" feels like a trusted friend guiding you through the maze of self-discovery. The 18 transformative principles are both practical and deeply resonant, addressing everything from gratitude practices to the art of letting go. Each chapter is infused with warmth and wisdom, making it easy to apply the concepts to my life. I particularly appreciated the emphasis on physical health's connection to mental well-being; it served as a wake-up call for me to prioritise my health. This book is an invaluable resource for anyone serious about personal growth!

Astrology Unveiled Series – "Profound, Logical, and Inspiring". What stands out in Astrology Unveiled is the author's dedication to making Vedic astrology logical and approachable. Each concept flows naturally into the next, backed by examples and exercises. The insights into karma and life cycles add a philosophical depth rarely seen in astrology books. Perfect for anyone seeking spiritual growth alongside astrological knowledge!

The Entitlement Trap - "Thought-Provoking and Challenging" The book challenges readers to confront their own sense of entitlement, and that's not easy—but it's essential. The Entitlement Trap doesn't offer a one-size-fits-all approach. Instead, it's a thoughtful, layered examination of how entitlement can limit our growth. The chapter on "Defining Your Own Hill" was particularly impactful, as it pushed me to reconsider which challenges are truly worth pursuing. A thought-provoking read for those willing to do the inner work to create a life they can be proud of.

Whispers of a Dying Soul – "A Soul-Stirring Reflection on Life's Unspoken Truths" - *Whispers of a Dying Soul: Unspoken Regrets and Unlived Dreams"* is a deeply moving exploration of the unexpressed emotions and unfulfilled aspirations that shape our lives in ways we often don't realise. This book invites readers to confront the powerful, often hidden impact of regret while guiding them through a journey of introspection and healing. Each page opens a space to reflect on the choices that define us—from moments of unspoken love to neglected passions—offering a gentle reminder to live authentically and courageously.

Whispers of the Soul: A Journey Through Haiku - is a mesmerising collection that speaks directly to the heart. Each haiku is a delicate brushstroke capturing life's fleeting beauty and timeless wisdom, inviting readers into moments of deep reflection and peace. This book is a balm for the soul, guiding us to find meaning in stillness and connection in simplicity. The themes of nature, love, and mindfulness echo universal truths, resonating with quiet, powerful grace. It's a book to be savoured slowly, cherished deeply, and returned to often. Truly, a gift for anyone seeking calm and clarity in life's chaos.

Whispers of Silence - Unlocking Inner Power through Stillness by Shree Shambav is a rare gem that beckons readers to pause, reflect, and reconnect with their inner selves. In a world that never stops talking, this book offers a profound exploration of silence—not as a void but as a rich and transformative space.

From the first page, Shree Shambav's writing resonates deeply, blending scientific insights with spiritual wisdom in a way that feels both universal and deeply personal. The author's ability to bridge the tangible and the transcendent makes this book an invaluable guide for anyone navigating the chaos of modern life.

The Power of Words: Transforming Speech, Transforming Lives - "The Power of Words is a profound and enlightening guide that has transformed the way I approach communication. Shree Shambav masterfully uncovers the hidden influence of our words on relationships, self-perception, and overall well-being. This book doesn't just teach you how to speak; it inspires mindful communication that fosters connection and trust. The insights on replacing negative patterns like gossip and judgment with kindness and authenticity are truly life-changing. The practical strategies and engaging narratives make it an invaluable resource for personal and professional growth. A must-read for anyone striving to communicate with intention, clarity, and compassion. Highly recommended!"

The Art of Intentional Living: Minimalism for a Life of Purpose - "The Art of Intentional Living is a refreshing guide to finding clarity in a cluttered world. With practical wisdom and profound insights, it inspires you to simplify, prioritise, and live with purpose. A must-read for anyone seeking balance and fulfilment."

Awakening the Infinite: The Power of Consciousness in Transforming Life - "Awakening the Infinite is a transformative guide that expands the mind and nourishes the soul. With profound insights and practical wisdom, this book beautifully explores the power of consciousness, helping readers connect with their true purpose and inner potential. It is a journey of self-discovery, healing, and spiritual awakening, offering clarity and inspiration at every turn. A must-read for anyone looking to live with greater awareness, meaning, and authenticity."

Beyond the Veil: A Journey Through Life After Death:

"This book touched me in ways few others have—it's not just about death, but about life, meaning, and the vast unknown that connects them. Beyond the Veil offers a graceful blend of science and spirit, inviting us to explore the mystery with awe rather than fear. The stories, insights, and reflections linger in your heart long after the final page. A truly transformative read that brings light on the shadows of mortality. It reminded me that in embracing death, we truly learn how to live."

Bonds Beyond Blood:

"A profoundly moving story that reminds us family is not defined by blood, but by love, sacrifice, and the courage to heal. Every chapter touched my soul with its emotional truth and timeless wisdom. Through joy, grief, and redemption, this book captures the raw beauty of human connection. I saw reflections of my own family in its pages—both the pain and the hope. A powerful, unforgettable read that lingers long after the final word."

A Journey into Spiritual Maturity: 12 Golden Rules for Inner Transformation

"This book is a gentle yet powerful guide that awakened a deeper sense of purpose within me. Each golden rule felt like a mirror reflecting truths I needed to embrace. Shree Shambav's wisdom is timeless, poetic, and profoundly grounding. It's not just a read—it's a journey into the heart of who you truly are. A must-read for anyone seeking lasting peace, clarity, and inner transformation."

The Inner Battlefield: Overcoming the Enemies of the Mind and Soul:

"This book is a powerful revelation—an honest mirror to the battles we fight within. Every chapter is a step closer to clarity, peace, and emotional mastery. Shree Shambav brilliantly transforms ancient wisdom into practical guidance for modern souls. It awakened in me a new strength to face my fears and rise above inner turmoil. A must-read for anyone seeking true inner victory and lasting transformation."

The Seeker's Gold – Unlocking Life's Greatest Treasure

The Seeker's Gold is a soul-stirring masterpiece that goes far beyond the pursuit of wealth—it is a journey into the heart of what truly matters. Each chapter unfolds with poetic wisdom and emotional depth, revealing that life's real treasure is not found in riches but in the transformation of the self. As the protagonist evolves through trials, love, and profound realisations, so does the reader. This book is a mirror for every dreamer, a lantern for every seeker, and a companion for anyone walking the path of purpose. A timeless tale that stays with you long after the final page.

Born to Rise Series I & II :

Born to Rise – Series I & II is a profound awakening—a journey that begins in silence and leads you to the core of your true power.

Series I reshapes your understanding of success, showing that clarity is more valuable than applause, and authenticity more powerful than performance.

Series II takes you deeper, unlocking the mindset and inner strategy behind meaningful, lasting growth—not just in wealth, but in wisdom.

Together, these books are not just guides—they are soul mirrors, revealing the truths you've forgotten and the strength you've always held.

This is more than reading—it's remembering who you are, and rising with purpose, not pressure.

ACKNOWLEDGEMENTS

To my grandfathers, grandmothers, mothers, fathers, aunts, uncles, neighbours, sisters, brothers, friends, and teachers, they poured in endless moral stories, retellings of Ramayana, Mahabharata, Puranas, Upanishads, and so on.

My teachers, neighbours, and kindred souls. Who provided us with a stage to perform wonderful Puranic stories and were gracious enough to acknowledge our efforts.

The artists and translators of epics have served as a source of inspiration, invigorating our spirits, making these works accessible, and enabling us to grasp the profound depths and deeper dimensions they contain.

I also cherish the stimulating conversations; I had with my wonderful mothers, Punitha Muniswamy and Uma Devi.

Our family's youngest member, Aadhya, who always overwhelmed me with questions, inspired this book.

I would likewise prefer to express gratitude to Mr Sivakumar, Mrs Roopa Sivakumar, Mr Akshaya Rajesh, Ms Akshatha Rajesh, Ms Apeksha Prabhu, Mr Akanksh Prabhu, Mr Nikash Sarasambi, and Mrs Spoorthi Nikash for their valuable inputs.

I must thank Mr Rajesh, Mr Savan Prabhu, Mrs Revathi Rajesh, Mrs Rajani Sarasambi, and Mrs Manju Reshma, who encouraged me and often suggested writing a book. Their unwavering belief that I had something valuable to offer kept me going during my writing sessions.

Love you all,

Shree Shambav

www.shambav.org

shreeshambav@gmail.com

www.ingramcontent.com/pod-product-compliance
Lightning Source LLC
LaVergne TN
LVHW091539070526
838199LV00002B/137